# FIDEL CASTRO

## OF CUBA

IN FOCUS BIOGRAPHIES

HAFIZ AL-ASAD OF SYRIA
BY CHARLES PATTERSON

ROBERT MUGABE OF ZIMBABWE
BY RICHARD WORTH

MARGARET THATCHER OF GREAT BRITAIN
BY MARIETTA D. MOSKIN

IN FOCUS

# FIDEL CASTRO
## OF CUBA

## JUDITH BENTLEY

JULIAN MESSNER

*I would like to acknowledge the help of Sara Sanchez
of South Seattle Community College and of
my daughter, Anne Bentley, in preparing this book.*

Copyright © 1991 by Judith Bentley
All rights reserved including the right of
reproduction in whole or in part in any form.
Published by Julian Messner, a division of
Silver Burdett Press, Inc., Simon & Schuster, Inc.
Prentice Hall Bldg., Englewood Cliffs, NJ 07632

JULIAN MESSNER and colophon are trademarks of
Simon & Schuster, Inc. Design by Leslie Bauman.
Manufactured in the United States of America.

Lib. ed.    10  9  8  7  6  5  4  3  2  1
Paper ed.   10  9  8  7  6  5  4  3  2  1

**Library of Congress Cataloging-in-Publication Data**

Bentley, Judith.
Fidel Castro of Cuba / by Judith Bentley.
p   cm. — (In focus biographies)
Includes bibliographical references (p.    ) and index.
Summary: Follows the life of the man who has been military
dictator of Cuba since 1959.
1. Castro, Fidel, 1927U–    —Juvenile literature.   2. Cuba—Politics
and government—1959–    —Juvenile literature.   3. Heads of state—
Cuba—Biography—Juvenile literature.   [1. Castro, Fidel,
1927–   .   2. Heads of state.]   I. Title.   II. Series.
F178.22.C3B46   1991
972.91'092—dc20
[B]                                              90-26057
ISBN 0-671-70198-3 (LSB)   ISBN 0-671-70199-1 (pbk.)   CIP
AC

# CONTENTS

# INTRODUCTION

For more than thirty years, ever since he appeared as a bearded guerrilla in the pages of *The New York Times*, Fidel Castro has been a world figure. He has made a revolution in Cuba, defeated a hated dictator, and replaced him with a Communist dictatorship. Then from the largest island in the Caribbean, a country only the size of the state of Pennsylvania, he has carved a place for himself and for Cuba in world politics. He has also encouraged Third World countries' struggles for independence and confronted the United States, only ninety miles away.

The revolution Castro brought into power is one of four major revolutions in Latin America during the twentieth century. (Mexico's revolution in 1910 and Bolivia's in 1954 took place before

Cuba's in 1959; Nicaragua's followed in 1979.) Yet Cuba's revolution has been the most radical and long-lived, mainly through the force of one man's personality.

Under Fidel's leadership, Cuba became a socialist state. Control of the economy was turned over to the national government, with Fidel at its head. The island nation was transformed from an underdeveloped country with a small, wealthy upper class and many living in poverty to a country in which everyone has a minimal but regulated standard of living. Cuba changed from a country dominated by the United States to a country dependent on the Soviet Union for economic support. From a country fearing invasion, Cuba became a country supporting wars and revolutions abroad. Cuba changed from a nation whose democratic principles existed in the constitution but not in practice to a nation whose individual rights are less important than the common good, as interpreted by Fidel.

In the 1990s, Castro still wears an olive-beige uniform like the one he wore during the revolution, but his curly beard is gray. He still shakes his fist against the "evils" of capitalism even as communism crumbles elsewhere. He has been in power longer than any other world leader today, but he may not continue to dominate Cuba. Castro attempted to make Cuba independent, and politically he succeeded. Economically, he has not succeeded. The standard of living in Cuba, although more equitable, has been falling.

This biography will trace Fidel's life from his boyhood in the 1920s to his position as *El Máximo Líder* in the 1990s. The success of his venture will be judged by the results of his more than thirty years in power, but first it must be judged against Cuba's history. Fidel brought together all the forces of rebellion and nationalism that had been brewing in Cuba since Christopher Columbus sailed onto the scene in 1492.

## "THE FAIREST ISLAND"

Columbus thought he had reached the Pacific islands of Japan when he landed on an island about 700 miles long and 25 to 130 miles wide. The natives called it Cubanacan, and it lay in the Caribbean Sea off the tip of what is now Florida. Columbus had found not Asia but a tropical treasure. Not only was the island "the fairest island human eyes have yet beheld," he wrote, but its brown-skinned inhabitants wore gold nuggets around their necks. When Columbus saw those nuggets, Cuba's fate was sealed. So was the fate of the native people. As Cuba became a colony of Spain, its inhabitants died of European diseases or in forced labor. Others died fighting Spanish armor, guns, and horses with their spears.

Columbus was disappointed in his search for gold, but in four hundred years of rule, the Spanish were not disappointed by the riches of Cuba. The Spanish colonizers used the island's fertile soil to raise sugarcane, cattle, and tobacco for export. Absentee land-owners lived in the largest city of Havana or even across the Atlantic in Spain while first the native Cubans and then African slaves worked the land. Havana's harbor became the main port for shipping goods between Spain and the New World. Inland the people learned to look out for themselves. Seeking to protect the wealth it gained from the island, Spain kept a tight grip on Cuba. By 1800 it was one of Spain's last colonies in North America.

## INDEPENDENCE FROM SPAIN

All Cuban schoolchildren now learn of the long struggle for independence from Spain, a struggle that began with the ringing of a bell on an October morning in 1868. Carlos Manuel de Céspedes, a fifty-year-old lawyer and plantation owner in Oriente province, had been involved in a plot against the Spanish. His plot was discovered by the authorities. Summoning his slaves with the bell, he told them they were free to join the war he was starting.

With fewer than forty men, Céspedes attacked Spanish forces in the town of Yara. After they were turned back, Céspedes's force was down to twelve men, but he said, "It doesn't matter. With twelve men I have enough to free Cuba." His proclamation from the town of Yara—"El grito de yara"—became the cry of freedom. Men flocked from all over Oriente to join him.

Within a month, twelve thousand Cubans were fighting for freedom and independence. Antonio Maceo, son of a free black, became one of the revolt's top military leaders. Known as the Bronze Titan, he used daring guerrilla tactics. Against much larger Spanish forces, Maceo made quick attacks from ambush and faded back into hiding in the countryside. He set up hospitals, workshops, food stores, and living areas for the rebels. By the spring of 1869 a temporary rebel government had been set up. At its peak this government controlled almost half of Cuba. As the war dragged on, however, the people suffered. The United States refused to recognize the rebels while selling arms to Spain. The rebels could defeat the Spanish sometimes, but they could not drive them from Cuba. Finally, what became known as the Ten Years War ended with a truce in February 1878.

The desire for freedom from Spain had not died, however. Early in the war, a sixteen-year-old youth name José Julián Martí had been arrested for "revolutionary sympathies." He had written a note to a fellow student accusing him of betraying the cause of all true Cubans by marching in a parade supporting the Spanish. Sentenced to hard labor in the stone quarries, Martí wore chains around his ankles for six months. Then friends of his father were able to have him freed and deported to Spain instead.

From then on, Martí devoted himself and his skills as a journalist, poet, writer, and lawyer to the cause of Cuban independence. Moving to New York City, he lived there for fifteen years and raised money for the Cuban Revolutionary party. In January 1895 he gave the order for a revolt to begin, with instructions that were rolled into a cigar and smuggled into Cuba. Uprisings started all over the island. They were led by Antonio Maceo and Máximo Gómez; Martí himself came ashore in a rowboat on the coast of Oriente. Only a month later he was killed when a group he had joined was betrayed by a Cuban guide and ambushed by Spanish soldiers. Maceo, too, was killed a year later. There would be no easy victory, but the names of the heroes of independence became embedded in the Cuban national memory.

The Spanish used harsh measures to put down the revolt. They sent a general the Cuban people called "the Butcher" because he forced them into concentration camps, where thousands starved to death. Although the United States refused to recognize the Cuban rebels, sentiment was growing for taking up arms on their side. When an American battleship, the *Maine*, exploded in Havana harbor in 1898, the United States blamed Spain and entered the war. Within four months Spain admitted defeat. It was exhausted by three years of guerrilla attacks and thirty years of rebellion.

With the Americans taking part, Cubans lost control of the war. They were shut out of the victory celebration; rebel troops were not even allowed into Havana. The Cuban Assembly was dissolved,  members of the revolutionary army disarmed, and no Cuban was present at the signing of the Treaty of Paris in December, ending the war. From 1899 to 1902 Cuba was occupied by U.S. military forces. Although the occupation accomplished some good, such as the eradication of the yellow fever spread by mosquitoes, the American presence was resented. The Platt Amendment, granting the United States two naval bases in Cuba and the right to intervene in Cuba's internal affairs, had been forced into the Cuban constitution. United States troops returned twice in the early 1900s when American interests were threatened.

Out of this history of harsh rule by the Spanish, years of rebellion, and interventions by the United States, Cuba's second century of revolution began. From years of struggle, a new revolutionary hero arose.

# 1

# BORN
# IN
# ORIENTE

Fidel Alejandro Castro Ruz was "born a guerrilla" in the middle of the night on August 13, 1927, in a house that stood on wooden piles amid a large sugarcane estate in Oriente province, Cuba. Fidel's entrance into the world was a grand one— he weighed 10 pounds, and his father, Ángel Castro y Argiz, was a wealthy farmer.*

Señor Castro's farm, "Las Manacas," was an odd place for a guerrilla to be born, for it was the lifelong work of a man who had grown wealthy in the shadow of the United Fruit Company. Fidel was Ángel's fifth child, the third by a Cuban peasant woman who was not yet his second wife. Although Fidel was born out of wedlock, his place in the village of Birán was unquestioned because his father owned most of it.

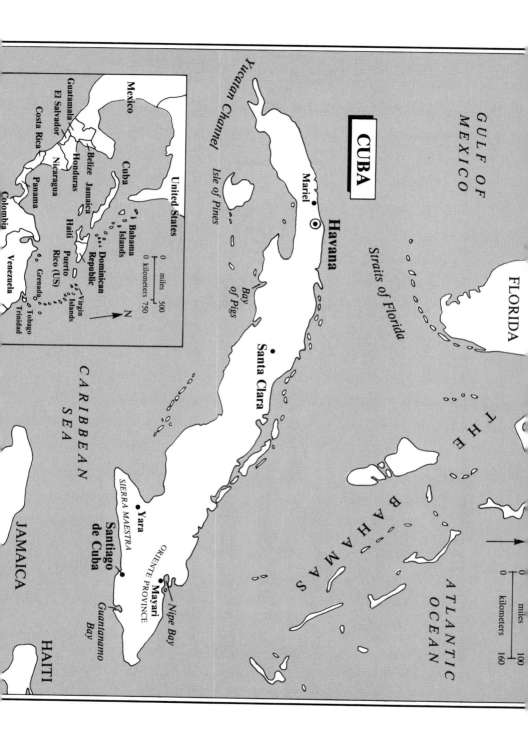

GULF OF
MEXICO

FLORIDA

CUBA

Straits of Florida

Yucatan Channel

Isle of Pines

Mariel

Havana

Bay
of Pigs

Santa Clara

THE

BAHAMAS

ATLANTIC
OCEAN

CARIBBEAN
SEA

SIERRA MAESTRA

Yara

Santiago
de Cuba

ORIENTE PROVINCE

Mayari

Nipe Bay

Guantanamo
Bay

JAMAICA

HAITI

0       miles      100
0   kilometers   160

Mexico

United States

Cuba

Guatemala
El Salvador
Costa Rica

Belize  Jamaica
Honduras
Nicaragua
Panama

Colombia

Venezuela

Bahama
Islands

Haiti

Dominican
Republic

Puerto
Rico (US)

Virgin
Islands

Grenada

Trinidad

Tobago

0      miles      500
0   kilometers   750

N

Oriente province, on the other hand, was the right place for a guerrilla to be born. It had a reputation for rebelliousness. Located on the southeastern tip of the island, the province was far from Spanish influence and control in Havana. The rural people who lived there were a mixture of mostly Spanish and African and thus regarded as truly Cuban people. Cuba's thirty-year war for independence had begun there in its mountain range, the Sierra Maestra. José Martí was killed in Oriente, barely twenty-five miles from where Fidel was born.

Fidel's father was of peasant stock. As a thirteen-year-old orphan, Ángel had come from Galicia, one of the poorest regions in Spain, to live with an uncle in the town of Santa Clara in central Cuba. This was soon after independence was won in 1898. After five years of working in a brickmaker's business, he struck out on his own to the Mayarí region in Oriente.

Mayarí's rich soil had been discovered by the American-owned United Fruit Company, which found the region ideal for planting sugarcane and tobacco and raising cattle. From Nipe Bay inland, the view was "an unbroken line of deep and velvety green . . . [an] ocean of growing sugarcane . . . as far as the eye can reach," one visitor observed. United Fruit had bought more than 315,000 acres in Mayarí and built several sugar mills and a railroad to the sea. The American company had become the region's main employer.

This foreign company provided the right opportunity for a strong, shrewd young man who was willing to work hard. Ángel worked in the nickel mines, did manual labor for United Fruit, and peddled merchandise in the countryside, using his profits from a small lemonade business. In time he organized and hired out a group of workers who cut trees for new sugar-planting fields, prepared the roadbeds for railroads, and transported loads of sugarcane to the large American-owned sugar companies. With the money from his work, he opened a small restaurant and bought a share in a clothing store.

As United Fruit expanded, Ángel, too, placed his peasant's faith in the value of the land and tapped into the growing Cuban dependence on sugar. At the age of thirty-five, he bought his own farm and began growing sugarcane. Señor Castro sold the sugarcane he grew to the large mills, known as *centrals.* The price he received was based on the price of sugar on the world market.

As the price of sugar rose before World War I, acres of Cuban forest were cleared and planted to cane. Prices could fall just as easily, however. In 1920 the price of sugar fell from 22.5 cents a pound to 3.58 cents. When that happened, more Cuban land was sold to American companies. Cuba's economic well-being gradually became dependent on sugar grown on foreign-owned land, milled in foreign-owned mills, shipped in United Fruit ships, and sold almost always to the United States.

"They came with bulging pockets to a nation impoverished [made poor] by thirty years of war, to buy the best land of this country for less than six dollars the hectare," Fidel Castro would later complain. Although a few men such as Ángel managed to prosper, most workers were very poor. Whereas American managers could go to company-run hospitals, schools, swimming pools, clubs, and stores filled with U.S. goods, thousands of cane cutters and mill workers lived with their families in *bohios,* or shacks. In the shadow of United Fruit lands, poor farmers and workers—illiterate, sick, often hungry—eked out a meager living. During the six months of the *zafra,* or growing season, they earned less than one dollar a day. For the rest of the year, they had nothing.

Fidel saw but did not experience such poverty. By the time he was born, Ángel owned and leased more than 23,000 acres, which he planted in sugarcane and sold to United Fruit's Miranda mill. He also grew fruit and raised cattle on the hilly areas. He owned a small nickel mine and a sawmill that processed lumber from the forested areas he leased. Eventually, every building in the village of Birán, except the post office and the school, belonged to Ángel.

Life in Birán was typical of Cuban peasant life in the first half of the twentieth century. Some three hundred families—one thousand people—lived and worked on the property. A few small farmers also grew sugarcane, but most were laborers, working for Ángel and growing food for themselves on small plots he gave them. Poorest of all were the Haitian workers, brought into the country by United Fruit to plant and cut the sugarcane and to work for lower wages than the Cubans. Their huts of palm thatch with dirt floors dotted the estate.

Although Ángel Castro was wealthy, he identified more with the peasants than with other landowners. Every day at dawn the tall figure in beard and wide-brimmed hat personally took breakfast to the cane cutters and planters in his fields. "No one went to bed there without eating ... ," his son Ramón has said, whereas on United Fruit lands, workers died of hunger. "But there were injustices ... My father was a very human man." His word was law, and he could be harsh to both his workers and his children.

Fidel inherited his father's height (Ángel was nearly six feet tall), his capacity for hard work, his strong will, and determination. Because they were such strong and similar personalities, father and son had frequent conflicts. Neither could tolerate authority.

Fidel's relationship with his mother was much warmer. Ángel married twice. His first wife, María Louisa Argote, is thought to have been an elementary-school teacher. Together they had two children who lived, Pedro Emilio and Lidia, before Ángel began an affair with a young maid in the household, Lina Ruz González.

María left, and three children—Ángela, Ramón, and Fidel— were born to Ángel and Lina before they were married in church. Raúl, Juana (called Juanita), Emma, and Agustina were born in the following years. Although Fidel seems to have suffered some embarrassment in his teens as a result of his birth out of wedlock, Cuban society as a whole is more tolerant of illegitimacy. "Remember we were children of love," Ramón explains.

Nearly illiterate, Lina taught herself to read and write. She had great hopes for her children and was determined that they would have an education.

Fidel Alejandro Castro Ruz was born in Cuba's Oriente province in 1927. Here he is shown kissing his mother, Lina. Fidel's father was a wealthy farmer.

## EARLY CHILDHOOD

Fidel's early childhood was generally happy. He lived in a large house, had nice clothes, and plenty to eat when other children were often hungry and "went barefoot while we wore shoes." Fidel spent long afternoons outdoors, running or riding horseback through the fields of the farm with his brothers and sisters. He grew into an athletic, adventurous child. He also loved to visit the sea, about twenty-five miles away, at Nipe Bay. There he spent hours with the fishermen, listening to their tales of struggles with sharks and whales.

From the beginning Fidel was a child who had to have his own way. Workers on the farm remember him as wild and unruly, with tremendous drive. Because of his father's position, his behavior was tolerated. "Everyone lavished attention on me, flattered and treated me differently from the other boys we played with when we were children," Fidel has told several biographers. He was more assertive and combative than the other children and knew how to get his way, with tantrums, manipulation, and violence if necessary. His sisters remember that he once organized a baseball team with bats, gloves, and equipment his father had ordered. With a good fastball but little control, Fidel preferred to be the pitcher. When his side was not winning, however, he stopped the game and went home.

Perhaps because they didn't know what else to do with him, his parents sent him with Raúl and Ángela to the local grammar school at the very young age of four. He soon learned to read and write. Despite being placed in the front row, where he could see the blackboard and listen to everything that was being said, his behavior was poor. "I spent most of my time being fresh....I remember that whenever I disagreed with something the teacher said to me, or whenever I got mad, I would swear at her and immediately leave school, running as fast as I could ... "

Besides learning to read and write, Fidel also developed a sensitivity to the suffering around him. The Castro children spent long periods of time with the Haitian cane cutters and often ate their meals with the workers. In a letter he wrote from prison in 1954, Fidel said that his classmates were the sons of humble peasants and generally came to school "barefoot and miserably clad ... They learned their ABC's very badly and soon dropped out of school, though they were endowed with more than enough intelligence." Without radical change, their future and their children's future promised only "a bottomless, hopeless sea of ignorance and poverty."

His brother Ramón agrees that Fidel's sympathy for the poor began on the large estate in Birán. "The latifundia [estate] was a school for Fidel. From his early years he saw the injustice.... To see children without food, [their parents] without jobs, that makes a man into a rebel."

---

*Spanish names contain the father's last name followed by the mother's last name. The shortened form drops the mother's name. The year of Fidel's birth was either 1926 or 1927. Fidel insists it was 1926, but there is some evidence that his birth record was set back a year when he was baptized and entered school.

# 2

# EDUCATED
# FOR THE
# ELITE

**W**hen Fidel was five or six years old, in the early 1930s, his parents decided to send him away from the village of Birán for a better education. He, his sister Ángela, and later his brother Ramón were sent to the city of Santiago de Cuba, the capital of Oriente. There they were to live with the sister of the Birán schoolteacher and receive special tutoring. Fidel is not sure whether he was sent away because he caused too much trouble at home or because the teacher convinced his family that it would be a good thing.

Whatever the reason, Fidel was miserable for the first two years in Santiago. Besides receiving little special instruction, other than rote memorization of addition, subtraction, multiplication, and division tables, the children also received little food. Fidel was home-sick and felt a deep sense of rejection by his parents. "I was taken from a world in which I lived without any material problems and taken to a city where I lived poorly and was hungry," he told the Brazilian priest Frei Betto fifty years later.

Fidel was not the only hungry child during the worldwide Depression of the early 1930s. Prices dropped and hunger and unemployment, particularly in the cities, were common. The price of sugar hit rock bottom in 1932—a half cent a pound—and many Cubans were thrown out of work. In the household of three adults in which the Castro children lived, only the schoolteacher had a job, and sometimes her pay was delayed or not paid at all. "We got a small container with a little rice, some beans, sweet potatoes and things like that.... I was always hungry."

During his second year in Santiago, Fidel's parents decided to enroll him and Ramón in the La Salle School. This was a school run by an order of Catholic priests to which many of Oriente's wealthy families sent their sons. While attending La Salle, Fidel continued to live with the schoolteacher's family.

In the first grade, Fidel entered a world of strict discipline and dress codes. Suits and ties were required at La Salle, but he enjoyed having professors, classes, and companions once again. He played a bugle in the school band, wearing his first uniform of navy blue with a white belt over his shoulder. By second grade the class photograph shows Fidel in the front row with a loose tie and a look of bored contempt on his face. A bright student, he managed to do well without working too hard.

Fidel was not happy being only a day student because he missed out on after-school outings, such as trips to the beach. He decided to do something about it by provoking a conflict with his guard-ians. When he was spanked for something, he began a campaign of rebellion, insulting everyone and shouting forbidden words. "I be-haved so terribly that they took me straight back to school and enrolled me as a boarder; it was a great victory for me."

## CUBA IN THE 1930s

Living in Santiago in the 1930s, Fidel witnessed some of the turmoil in urban Cuba. Standing opposite the public high school one day, he saw a group of students come out and walk past some Cuban sailors carrying guns. "They must have muttered something to the sailors because they had walked only a little way when the sailors followed them into the building, brought them out, and took them off to jail, hitting them with their gun butts. This left a lasting impression on me," he told Carlos Franqui, a rebel journalist.

Tensions were high between secondary students, soldiers, and sailors. For thirty years, since the U.S. occupation ended in 1902, a succession of presidents had ruled Cuba, mostly in a dictatorial and undemocratic fashion. To gain and hold power, a politician needed support from the United States, which wanted stability and order. Once in power, a president would grant jobs and privileges to his followers. Corruption became a tradition in Cuban politics. The latest president, Gerardo Machado y Morales, had been elected in 1924 on the promise of reform, but he had extended his term, been reelected with no opposition, and become a virtual dictator. After nine years of such rule, students, workers, the young Communist party, and older political leaders opposed him with protests, strikes, and bombs.

"I used to sleep on a small sofa near the back door," Fidel says, "and at night the bombs exploding close by would wake me up."

In the summer of 1933 Machado was forced to resign after a general strike, pressure from the United States, and a timely military overthrow led by a little-known Cuban army sergeant, Fulgencio Batista. For one hundred days, Cuba had a truly reform government, first under a council of five men and then under Ramón Grau San Martín. Grau was unable to pull the many political groups together, however, or to gain recognition from the United States. The spirit of reform weakened; a man more acceptable to U.S. interests, Carlos Mendieta, was named president. In fact, Batista held the real power.

Two years later opposition erupted again. Elementary-school teachers began a protest against the government's neglect of education. The protest quickly spread and became a general strike, but Batista threw the army's weight against the strikers. Military firing squads executed civilians, and the student generation of the 1930s was thrown into jail, sent into exile, or silenced. Not until Fidel's college generation of the 1940s would students dare to challenge the government again.

## REBELLIONS IN SCHOOL

The boy Fidel continued his own personal rebellion against authority and his classmates at La Salle. His brother Raúl says that he fought every day, defying the most powerful and the strongest. "[When] he was beaten he began again the next day. He never gave up."

Once he gave a black eye to a boy who was favored by the priests. A priest called Fidel into his office, slapped him across his face, catching him on the other cheek with his backhand. Fidel remembers feeling painfully humiliated. Ángel received reports that his boys were bullies and didn't study, so he decided not to send them back after fourth grade. Fidel angrily protested to his mother that he wanted to go on studying and it wasn't fair not to let him go to school. When he threatened to set fire to the house if he wasn't sent back, they decided to let him go.

When Fidel went back to complete fifth grade, he was transferred to the Colegio Dolores, a school run by the Jesuits. Dolores set very high standards. Despite some early difficulties with the schoolwork, Fidel was a promising athlete who played soccer, basketball, and jai alai, a game like handball played with a curved basket. These abilities made him popular, but his indifference to clean clothes earned him the nickname "Bola de Churre" (dirtball).

One Sunday during an outing, the priest punished two students by not allowing them to go swimming. Fidel proposed a deal: "If I dive down from the ten-meter board, will you let them swim?" The priest protested that the board was too high, but he agreed, and Fidel jumped, proving his courage and winning a privilege for his classmates.

Fidel was a day student again. This time he boarded with a merchant's family who would shut him up in his room for hours after school to study. Fidel used this time to stage make-believe historical battles instead. "I'd start off by taking a lot of little scraps and tiny balls of paper, arranging them on a playing board, and setting up an obstacle to see how many would pass and how many wouldn't. There were losses, casualties. I played this game of wars for hours."

When he could not stand his guardian's home any longer, Fidel staged another confrontation, recounted in a biography by Tad Szulc. "I decided to create a situation in which they had no alternative but to send me to school as a boarder. From then on I definitely became my own master and took charge of all my own problems without advice from anyone." His years of schooling away from home taught him self-reliance and gave him a strong sense of self-confidence.

## CORRUPTION IN POLITICS

Most summers Fidel returned home and passed the time climbing hills, swimming in the Birán River, riding horses, and hunting with a shotgun and a pack of four dogs. He had an appetite for the outdoors. On the estate he also had a firsthand look at how elections were won. During one campaign Fidel remembers political captains arriving early in the morning to be given money from his father's safe, which was kept in the room where the boy slept.

"A lot of money circulated in my house at election time. That's what politics was like then. Of course, as a landowner, my father controlled most of the votes. . . . To be given a job in the rural areas was considered a big favor then, as was being allowed to live on somebody else's land. Therefore, the farmer or worker for whom such a favor was done—and all the rest of his family—had to be grateful to the patron and vote for his candidate. . . . I formed a very poor opinion of all this," Castro told Frei Betto.

Fidel was not the only one with a poor opinion of politics run through corruption. After the failed strike of 1935, the reform spirit had died, and several weak presidents were dominated by Batista. President Franklin D. Roosevelt canceled the Platt Amendment, by which the United States had kept the right to intervene in Cuban affairs. The United States solidly supported the Batista regime, however, because it provided a stable environment for U.S. investment. Batista sponsored some welfare plans to win popular support, and he met some of labor's demands for pensions, a minimum wage, and limited working hours. He also made an effort to improve the health and educational level of the rural poor, but he enlarged the army. The police felt free to push people around and the army to assassinate opponents.

In 1940, responding to political pressure, Batista allowed the election of delegates to a convention that wrote a new constitution for Cuba. This was the Constitution of 1940. It contained many of the reforms asked for by the student generation of the 1930s. The president was limited to one term of four years. Freedom of speech and press, freedom of criticism and assembly, and the right of the people to rebel against government violation of the constitution were protected. The government was given a strong role in providing jobs for citizens and was required to use the country's natural resources for the social good; the University of Havana was guaranteed independence from the government; workers were guaranteed paid vacations, a minimum wage, and job tenure; and Cubans were to be favored over foreigners in the establishment of new industries.

The new constitution sounded good, but many of its reforms were never enforced. Moreover, Batista completely disregarded the new constitution and rigged the presidential elections so that he was elected in 1940.

## A JESUIT EDUCATION

In the early 1940s Fidel graduated from Dolores with a determination to excel and distinguish himself. He would spend the last two years of his high school education in an even more elite school, the Jesuit-run school at Colegio Belén in Havana.

Fidel had outgrown fighting, but at Belén, too, he had to prove himself. Soon after arriving, he rode a bicycle full-speed into a brick wall, just to prove he had the willpower to do things others would never dare to do. His athletic activities continued. "I played everything," he recalled. "I always liked sports a lot. For me, they served as a diversion, and I put my energy into them." In 1944 Fidel was voted the "best school athlete" in Cuba. The Washington Senators thought enough of his pitching skills to give him a tryout, but professional baseball was not to be his career.

He also became an excellent debater and a good student, putting his amazing memory, tenacity, and determination to work for him. "He wrote everything exactly the way he read it," a classmate comments, "and it looked as if he had copied it, but he had it all engraved in his memory. And he got good grades for his fantastic memory."

He concentrated on the subjects that interested him: agriculture, Spanish, sociology, geography, and history, paying special attention to the lives of strong figures like Julius Caesar and Benito Mussolini, their exercise of power and ability to shape events. He became familiar with the life and writings of José Martí. Fidel was also fascinated by the Bible, the stories of Moses, Joshua, Samson, and "all the wars and battles." The religious training, however, he found too strict. The annual three-day religious retreats—times of silent prayer—were especially "cruel" for a young man who liked to talk.

The Jesuits tamed his rebelliousness but not his will to pursue any goal he set. He joined the Explorers, a Jesuit organization similar to the Boy Scouts, which had its own uniforms and went on

This photograph from his 1945 high school yearbook shows Fidel making a speech.

camping trips in the mountains. Fidel became the leader of the troop and was known for his stamina and endurance.

When he graduated in the top ten of his class, Fidel's yearbook entry said he had an excellent record, "always defending with bravery and pride the flag of the school. He has known how to win the admiration and affection of all. He will make law his career and we do not doubt that he will fill with brilliant pages the book of his life. He has good timber and the actor in him will not be lacking."

His Jesuit teachers saw Fidel as a boy with great talent and leadership potential, despite his rural background. After Belén, Fidel could have taken his place in the Cuban upper class, but he did not choose that route. The priests taught him how to think. They taught him self-discipline, endurance, and a strong sense of personal dignity, honor, and duty. In 1945 he lacked only political awareness and a suitable arena for his ambition.

CHAPTER

# 3

# A YOUNG VOLCANO

On entering the University of Havana in the fall of 1945, Castro found that his fellow students were not very idealistic. Students of the 1930s had helped overturn a dictator, Machado, but had seen their hopes for an honest, nationalistic, and democratic government dashed. In the ten years since then, Batista, as commander in chief of the armed forces and then president from 1940 to 1944, had become rich through racketeering in gambling and prostitution. Havana became a playground for rich American tourists and businessmen while many Cubans lived in poverty.

When Batista retired temporarily to his mansion in Florida in 1944, he was succeeded by Grau San Martín, who had governed

**30**

briefly after the overthrow of Machado. Cuban voters hoped Grau would continue the reforms he had begun then, but he had lost his fire. Like many presidents before him, Grau, too, became more interested in his personal power and wealth then in bringing about change for the benefit of all Cubans.

More importantly for Castro, Grau was unable to control student gangsters who had replaced the idealistic student leaders on the University of Havana campus. These *pistoleros* had revolutionary sounding names—Movimiento Socialista Revolucionaria (MSR) and Unión Insurrecional Revolucionaria (UIR)—but they were really just hired guns. During Grau's four-year term, these gangs carried out sixty-four political assassinations. Since police were forbidden by the constitution to enter the campus, it became a haven for the *pistoleros*. Student leaders spent as much time taking part in the gangs' activities or in politics as they did in studying.

Into such chaos strode a tall, intense, politically ambitious, talkative young man wearing a dark suit and tie. At first sight, Castro looked like a son of the ruling class. "I was in a panic," recounts Alfredo Guevara, a staunch Communist who would become Fidel's close friend. "Here was this Castro dressed up fit to kill in his black party suit, handsome, self-assured, aggressive, and obviously a leader. He had come out of Belén parochial school, and I saw him as a political threat."

Castro was not, of course, a conservative, upper-class product of his Jesuit education. He was the rebellious son of a rural landowner who had not been involved in politics at Belén. Wearing a suit, in contrast to the more common *guayabera* or sports shirt, may have been an attempt to compensate for his Oriente background. Fidel settled into a boarding house in the university district, enrolled in the law school, and started searching for politics that would fit his personality and background.

His aim at first was to become president of the Federation of University Students, abbreviated FEU from its name in Spanish, which held elections a few weeks after the term began. Fidel was elected the delegate from his legal anthropology course and then representative of the freshman class, but he could go no further. None of the politically organized student groups would risk supporting him because he was too unreliable and unpredictable. Fidel could never be elected president of the law school, a fellow student said, because he would not work with others. Likewise, representatives of both MSR and UIR tried to enlist him, but he kept an independent stance. He was never one to submit to any party's discipline unless he could be its head.

## A POLITICAL CAREER BEGINS

Nevertheless, Castro quickly gained a personal following. Serious, well-spoken, powerfully built, excitable, he had a presence that attracted other politically minded students. He spent hours at a café, as recounted by Max Lesnick in several biographies of Castro. "He talked politics all the time, *all* the time, with a very, very grandiose and at the same time idealistic scheme of how to run the country, how to improve things. He did it with a great deal of passion, emotion, vehemence [force]—convincing people. He had that capacity. . . . Fidel was the only one who could instantly mobilize [gather] fifty persons to follow him, and when he could not get students, he went out to chase followers in the streets." In constant motion, he was also regarded as a little crazy at the time because he had great ambition and grand fantasies.

With such an active political life, Castro was too busy to study much or socialize. Through cramming and using his sharp memory and keen mind, he was able to pass his exams at the end of the first year and to pass most courses with honors. However, his studies always took a back seat to politics. He never went to dancing and drinking spots. Indeed, the idea of Fidel dancing was "inconceivable" to his friends.

Castro had entered the university without any knowledge of politics, bringing only his rebellious temperament and intellectual curiosity. He used his university years to read widely, beginning with the history and heroes of Cuba: Antonio Maceo, Máximo Gómez,

Carlos Manuel de Céspedes, and especially the poet and independence fighter José Martí. Castro read volumes of Martí's work and used Martí quotes in his speeches. Fidel found much to admire in the idealist who always sided with the poor.

"I will stake my fate on the poor of the earth," Martí had written. He called for granting land to those who farmed it and a better distribution of the national wealth. He said it is the government's duty to provide education, and he urged direct vote elections. Martí dreamed of a just society free of foreign domination, racism, and the power of wealth and big business.

In addition to reading Martí, Fidel studied political economics, looking for answers to society's problems. He was particularly disturbed by the cycles of unemployment he saw in capitalist societies. Why, he wondered, should unemployed workers in England freeze while there was plenty of coal in the ground? Why must cane workers in Cuba suffer through months of the "dead season" between harvests, living on cornmeal and *guarapo*, the juice of sugarcane?

Castro found some answers in books by Lenin, Engels, and Marxz, the "fathers" of modern communism, which he bought on credit at the Communist party bookstore. Studying Marx helped him understand the class divisions, he said. He was impressed with Marx's statement that 10 percent of capitalist society lives on the work of the other 90 percent.

Although Castro was becoming at least a socialist in his thought, he did not join the Communist party. The Cuban Communist party was a small group in the 1940s, but it had dominated the labor unions since the early 1930s and had been legalized in 1939. One reason Castro may have avoided the party was that it supported Batista. Another obstacle was its rigid discipline and hierarchy. Borrowing from both Martí and Marx, Castro forged his own revolutionary stance.

Castro's reading led him away from his goals of being elected to student government and toward more involvement in national politics. In November 1946, barely nineteen, he made his debut as a speaker on the seventy-fifth anniversary of the execution of eight medical students for allegedly dishonoring a Spaniard's grave. In his speech, Castro attacked the Grau government and called Cubans to rise against those who allowed them to starve to death. Parts of the speech made the front page of the Havana newspapers the next day.

Castro's increasing outspokenness attracted the attention of gangster Mario Salabarria Aguilar, who was also the chief of the secret police. Salabarria warned Castro to stop his criticism of the Grau administration and of gangs or to get off campus for good. Recognizing the threat to his political career, if not to his life, Fidel left the university district for a few days and went to a beach near Havana to think. Never lacking in physical courage, he decided he would rather die a hero than back down. "Not to return would be to give in to threats, to give in before bullies, to abandon my own ideals and aspirations [hopes], so I decided to go back," he related, but he did so armed with a gun. Fidel has said that his years at the university were more physically dangerous than his years in guerrilla warfare in the Sierra Maestra.

From 1947 on, Fidel was a young man in constant motion, a "volcano," erupting as occasions for public speech-making arose. That spring a political party, the Ortodoxo party, was formed to organize against Grau, claiming that it stood for loyalty to the ideals of Martí. Led by Eduardo "Eddy" Chibás, a charismatic, idealistic congressman and former student leader of the 1930s, the Ortodoxos soon attracted a following among youth. Indeed, Castro was at the founding assembly, and he worked within the party for the next eight years. Chibás began giving weekly Sunday radio talks in which he exposed graft and corruption in high places, attacked Grau's leadership, and called for reform.

Castro, too, took every chance to attack the government. That fall a high school student was shot at a rally by a bodyguard of the education minister. Several thousand students chanting "Down with Grau" marched past the Presidential Palace. Fidel was in the front ranks, helping to carry the student's flag-draped coffin. After thousands more from the working-class district joined the marchers, Fidel spoke to the crowd from the *escalinata*, the large central staircase of the university. He lashed out at the *pistoleros* and blamed Grau for the shooting.

Castro did not limit himself to mere words when a chance for heroic action arose. Rafael Trujillo was the type of dictator Latin American students loved to hate. Since 1930 he had ruled the Dominican Republic with an iron hand. Trujillo allowed foreign-owned companies to dominate the economy while enriching himself. A group of Dominican exiles and Cubans, apparently with the backing of the Grau government, planned an invasion to bring him down. Fidel was an eager recruit. After two months of training and waiting, however, the expedition was called off.

When he returned for his third year of law school in the fall of 1947, Castro was even more intent on working to overthrow Grau. With this goal in mind, he chose to audit classes rather than officially enroll. In November he planned a large meeting that would confront Grau and demand his resignation. The meeting was to take place on the eightieth anniversary of the beginning of Cuba's struggle for independence. To honor that date, the president wanted to bring to Havana the bell Carlos Manuel de Céspedes rang to gather his rebels. The sugarcane workers and Communist mayor of the town where the bell rested turned Grau down. However, Fidel persuaded them to let him bring it to Havana instead. The three-hundred-pound bell was taken by train and then by car through the streets of Havana to the university. The huge demonstration and ringing of the bell were planned for the next day, but during the night the bell disappeared. Castro suspected Grau or the *pistoleros* of seizing it.

Foiled in that attempt to bring about a confrontation, Castro also observed later that year that revolutions do not occur without careful planning. As a Cold War developed between the United States and the Soviet Union after World War II, the United States tried to strengthen its influence in Latin America by setting up a regional organization, the Organization of American States (OAS). Latin

American leaders were expected to sign the OAS charter during the Ninth Inter-American Conference in Bogotá, Colombia, in the spring of 1948. Leftist students, including Fidel, saw the conference as a chance to organize a student congress. The purpose of the student congress would be to oppose U.S. foreign policy in Latin America. Several Cuban students were flown to Bogotá for the congress, at the expense of the Argentinian government of Juan Perón.

Before the conference began, Castro and other Cuban students met with Colombia's popular Liberal party leader, Jorge Eliécer Gaitán. They asked him to deliver the closing speech at the student congress. The next day Castro was walking toward a second meeting with Gaitán when people rushed past him shouting, "They killed Gaitán!" The Liberal party leader had been murdered while crossing a street in front of his hotel. The people blamed the Conservative government for Gaitán's death, and a wave of fierce street fighting and urban revolt followed. Known as the Bogotazo, this riot resulted in the killing of 3,600 people in one day. Most of the killing was done by government forces.

Fidel joined the revolt, but he was dismayed by the Liberals' lack of leadership as the people rioted and looted after Gaitán's murder. In Castro's view, any chance for seizing power and making radical changes was lost without strong leaders and politically aware masses. An agreement was soon reached to end the fighting. After that, the president of Colombia denounced the Cuban students in Bogotá as "Communists." Fidel and his companions were flown back to Havana on a cargo plane. The Bogotá experience gave Castro an undying hatred for the OAS, whose purpose, he thought, was to put down popular revolutions in Latin America. He also saw how quickly leftists could be labeled Communists.

## OBSESSED WITH REVOLUTION

When he returned to Havana, Fidel continued to be obsessed by revolution. He talked about it without end. Eddy Chibás was running for president, and Fidel threw himself into the final phase of Chibás's campagin, accompanying him on a trip through Oriente. Chibás used a broom to symbolize the sweeping away of corruption. His motto was *"verguenza contra dinero"*—honor versus money. Despite his efforts, Chibás was defeated in June by Carlos Prío Socarrás, who quickly became as corrupt a president as Grau.

Two days after Prió took office in the fall of 1948, Fidel was married to a small, dark-eyed philosophy student he had met through a friend in the law school. Mirta Díaz-Balart was the daughter of a wealthy family in Oriente. Mirta's family did not approve of Fidel's politics. Nevertheless, she was very much in love with Fidel, and they were married in the Roman Catholic Church in Banes, not far from Birán. Ángel Castro was delighted with the marriage and paid for a honeymoon of several weeks in the United States.

Back in Havana, the young couple settled into a modest hotel a block from the university. Fidel was too taken up with politics and dreams of revolution to give much attention to his marriage, however. While in Havana, he and Mirta became parents of a son. Fidel Castro Díaz-Balart, called "Fidelito," was born September 1, 1949. In his last two years of law school Fidel took part in several violent protests, then skipped classes in the spring and summer of 1950 to prepare for exams. In six months he covered a two-year workload and graduated the following September with a Doctor of Law, Doctor of Social Sciences, and Doctor of Diplomatic Law.

Castro's years at the University of Havana had made him a revolutionary in thought and in goals. He also gained valuable speaking and leadership skills. Most of all, Castro had become convinced of the need for a complete social revolution in Cuban society that would erase the differences between rich and poor.

Upon graduating, Fidel started a "poverty-law" firm with two other lawyers. Their tiny office was located on the second floor of a rundown building in an old section of Havana. Although his wife's family connections could have gained him more income, Fidel chose to take the cases of poor people who could seldom afford their legal bills. Usually Castro accepted no fees; he and Mirta were constantly in debt, sometimes surviving on money from his father.

In August 1951 during his popular weekly radio program, Eddy Chibás called on the Cuban people to awake, then shot himself in the stomach. He developed a massive infection and died a few days later. Fidel was at his bedside. The emotional response of the people to Chibás's death seemed likely to carry the Ortodoxos to victory in the 1952 spring presidential elections. So Castro decided to run as an Ortodoxo for a seat in the House of Representatives. If elected, he promised to urge farmers, workers, unemployed teachers, intellectuals, and others to launch a revolutionary movement. Castro ran a strong, grass-roots campaign. He bought radio time and gained newspaper coverage for accusations of corruption against Prío. The candidate provided a list of more than two thousand monthly government paychecks that went to members of the pistolero groups.

Thus Fidel had a reasonable hope of being elected to the House of Representatives in June. Into the picture stepped Fulgencio Batista, who had been allowed to return to Cuba that year and run for president. Batista, however, did not expect to win. On the morning of March 10, 1952, he strutted into Camp Columbia, the army camp in Havana, and took command from officers who had already prepared a takeover of the government. Cuba's hope for democracy and Fidel's chance for an elected political career were gone.

# 4

# INVITATION
# TO
# REVOLUTION

A fter Batista's takeover, a feeling of pessimism and sadness overcame Cuba. Democratic government in Cuba had taken a step backward, and no effective opposition arose. The FEU was ready to respond, and ousted president Prío had promised them arms, but he fled the country instead. The United States immediately recognized Batista, preferring a "strong man" dictatorship that was friendly and anti-Communist to an unstable democracy.

Under Batista's rule in both the 1940s and the 1950s, some improvements were made. New tourist centers were developed, public works projects completed, gang violence eliminated, the cattle industry and mining sector expanded. With U.S. arms and money supporting order, business flourished. Cuba's industries brought large profits to both U.S. and Cuban investors. Still, Cuban workers earned low wages and industries paid low taxes to the Cuban government. Gradually, Cuban ownership of the sugar mills grew, increasing from 22 percent of the mills in 1939 to 55 percent in 1952. American businesses, however, still controlled 90 percent of Cuban utilities, such as telephones and electricity, and 50 percent of the railroads. Cuba's beaches, luxurious resort hotels like the Havana Hilton, and elegant gambling casinos attracted the rich, usually North Americans. Smuggling and other illegal activities were widespread. By 1954 the wealthy residents of Havana bought more Cadillacs than residents in any other city in the world.

The temporary stability that allowed a few to become wealthy and made Cuba "safe" for tourists was bought with force, strict censorship, and the use of secret police. Anyone suspected of opposition to the government was thrown into jail, exiled, and often tortured. Some opponents were executed. Batista and his police were responsible for twenty thousand murders.

Economically, Cuba remained inherently unstable. Sugar accounted for 85 percent of exports, and its production depended on a workforce of 600,000 who became unemployed during the "dead season." Cuba's main customer, the United States, insisted on low Cuban tariffs on imported manufactured goods. This policy discouraged growth of the island's own manufacturing.

Most serious was the gap between the rich and the poor. Many big landowners, businessmen, high government officials and military officers, top-ranking politicians, and successful professionals had acquired their wealth or position through corruption. Although the overall living standard was relatively high for Latin America, cane cutters made only one to two dollars for a ten-hour day cutting cane. *Campesinos* were lucky to live past the age of forty; they were malnourished, landless, and illiterate. Only 11 percent of Cubans living in the countryside in the 1950s drank milk, barely 4 percent ate beef, and only 2 percent ate eggs. Eight percent of the landowners owned 70 percent of the land. In Castro's home region of

Cuban cane cutters had work during the sugarcane harvest but were mainly unemployed during the "dead season." They were among the poorest of the poor.

Mayarí, only about half the population over the age of six had attended even the first grade.

Such conditions invited revolution. Looking back on that period, American historian Arthur Schlesinger, Jr., told the United States State Department in 1961 that "the character of the Batista regime in Cuba made a violent popular reaction almost inevitable. The rapacity [greed] of the leadership, the corruption of the Government, the brutality of the police, the regime's indifference to the needs of the people for education, medical care, housing, for social justice and economic opportunity—all these, in Cuba as elsewhere, constituted an open invitation to revolution." The invitation needed only a man who was willing to take on Batista.

Castro was not only publicly outraged by Batista's coup but personally angry, too. A military dictatorship now stood in the way of his own political plans. Although most Cubans just wanted a return to representative democracy, Fidel wanted to make a social revolution that would equalize the wealth.

The day of Batista's coup, Castro first went to the university campus to await the arms promised by Prío. Then in the afternoon he and a few Ortodoxo members left for a small farm outside Havana where they wrote a manifesto, or public declaration, denouncing Batista. The manifesto ended with a challenge to take up opposition to the dictator, using words from Martí and the Cuban national anthem: "To live in chains is to live in shame."

No established politicians from the older generation took up the challenge, but at a political rally that spring, Castro met a small group of young activists who owned a mimeograph machine and had already published an anti-Batista pamphlet. Abel Santamaría, a twenty-four-year-old accountant at an automobile dealership, and his sister Haydée shared a tiny apartment that had become a center of revolutionary talk. After just a few visits to the apartment, it was clear that Castro would be the leader of the young people and Abel the second-in-command.

"I think this happened to everybody," said Melba Hernández, a lawyer member of the group. "From the moment you shake hands with Fidel you are impressed. His personality is too strong."

With this core of eight to ten, Fidel began recruiting for the "Centennial Generation," the generation that would start a revolution in 1953, the one hundredth anniversary year of Martí's birth. Although Fidel had become known as a student leader, he recruited the earnest young working-class people in the lowest-income areas of Havana and other cities. Eventually, Fidel had twelve hundred men.

One student demonstration after another challenged Batista as the older political leadership sought compromises. "You can't count on these politicians to make a revolution," Fidel exclaimed as he walked out of an Ortodoxo meeting in January. Neither could you count on the students, who were always willing to protest but lacked the discipline for a long-term opposition. In April 1953 the National Revolutionary Movement (MNR), led by university professor Rafael García Bárcena, attempted to overthrow Batista by attacking Camp Columbia. Their plan was common knowledge, however, and they were arrested before they began.

Castro had a different plan in mind. He had enough men for a successful military action but few weapons and little money to buy them. Instead, he decided to capture them by attacking the Moncada army barracks in Santiago, the second largest military base in Cuba. A simultaneous attack would be made on the Bayamo barracks to the northwest of Santiago on the western approaches to the Sierra Maestra. A farm was bought in Siboney, ten miles outside Santiago, for the purpose of "raising chickens." Castro chose 170 of his best fighters and sent them in small groups to Siboney.

## AN ATTACK FAILS

To the men crowded into the mattress-lined living room of the darkened farmhouse on the night of July 25, 1953, Fidel revealed the object and plan of the attack. "Comrades, tomorrow we may win or we may lose," he told them, "but in the end this movement will triumph. If we win, tomorrow will fulfill what Martí aspired to. If we don't, the gesture will have set an example for the people of Cuba." Although the attackers would be outgunned and out-manned, Fidel thought that the fort could be taken without firing a shot. If not, he seemed willing to die a hero's death.

A cavalcade of fifteen cars left the farmhouse before dawn. They would divide into three groups. The main group under Fidel's command would enter the complex of buildings through Guard Post 3. The other two, under Abel Santamaría and Raúl Castro, would seize a hospital and a rooftop commanding access to the barracks ground. (Raúl had just graduated from the university, joined the Young Communists, and then the assault on Moncada out of loyalty to his brother.) Abel and Raúl achieved their objectives, but Fidel's group met a passing patrol just as they had disarmed the guards at the post. A shot was fired, the barracks were alarmed, and the element of surprise was gone with only the first carload of attackers inside the gates.

The battle lasted only a half hour, killing eight rebels and nine-teen soldiers, before Fidel ordered a retreat. Raúl's group retreated, but Abel's group of nineteen men, his sister Haydée, and Melba Hernández kept firing until they were out of ammunition and were captured. The rest of the Moncadistas fled in cars or on foot through the streets, quickly shedding the homemade uniforms they had worn as a disguise to gain entry. The smaller attack on Bayamo lasted only ten minutes and also failed.

More of the rebels died after the attack than during it. About sixty rebels escaped, but ninety-one were taken prisoner and two-thirds of them, including Abel, were killed in prison in the next few days, often after cruel torture. Hearing the screams and seeing the bodies, the people of Santiago asked their archbishop to intervene, which he did, gaining a published promise from the commanding officer that the murder of prisoners would stop.

Fidel was among those who escaped early capture. Five days after the attack he and a few companions were trying to reach the Sierras. They had sought shelter from the mist and cold and were sleeping in a thatched-roof shed. Castro recounted that he woke up with a patrol's rifles in his chest, a "most disagreeable sensation." The soldiers of the patrol were ready to kill him despite the agreement with the archbishop, but the lieutenant-in-command intervened.

Although the Moncada attack was a military failure, it was a strategic success because it aroused public support. Thousands of Santiago citizens attended a solemn mass for the rebels who had been killed. When the survivors went on trial in September 1953, Castro proved himself to be more dangerous with words than he had been with weapons. For the first few days, acting as his own lawyer, he turned the trial into a cross-examination of the killing of prisoners and the Batista regime. So effective were his arguments that his jailers told the judge he was ill, and his trial was moved to a small nurses' lounge in the hospital. There, in a stiflingly hot room, he gave a two-hour summation of the legitimacy of the attack, closing defiantly with the words, "Condemn me. It does not matter. History will absolve [acquit] me."

The speech that became known as "History Will Absolve Me" provides an important outline of the social revolution Castro had in mind. With quotes from philosophers and religious leaders and from the Declaration of Independence, Castro made some promises. He would give ownership of small farms to the *campesinos* and a share of profits from work to the workers. He would promote industrial development and eliminate unemployment. He would nationalize, or have the Cuban government take over, the American-owned electric and telephone companies. To farm laborers living in miserable shacks, he would provide public housing and to urban workers a 50 percent reduction in rents. Improvements in education and health would confront the problems of illiteracy, malnutrition, and disease. He made other promises, too, such as restoration of the Constitution of 1940, elections, a free press, free speech, an independent judiciary, and an end to the practice of buying arms.

## TO PRISON

After the silence that followed Castro's speech, the judge sentenced him to fifteen years in prison on the Isle of Pines, an island off the southwestern coast of Cuba. Raúl was sentenced to thirteen years, twenty-six other men and the two women to lesser terms.

In prison, Fidel at first spent his time on the political education of the surviving Moncadistas, using one hundred of his books, which he sent for. In addition to books, friends sent him food and a large number of lemons, for Fidel was determined that "History Will Absolve Me" reach the public. He wrote to his followers that the next step was "to get public opinion behind us, make our ideas known and win the support of the masses." By writing in lemon juice between the lines of letters and by sending out sentences in the false bottoms of matchboxes, he was able to smuggle out the complete text of the speech over a three-month period. Melba Hernández and Haydée Santamaría, who had been released, collected the letters and used a hot iron to bring out the brown tracing of the words left by the lemon juice. They printed ten thousand pamphlets of the speech, which was distributed from town to town in an old car.

In mid-April of 1954 Batista visited the prison to attend a ceremony inaugurating a power plant at the prison. Fidel persuaded his men, the imprisoned Moncadistas, to serenade Batista with "The 26th of July March," a hymn Castro had commissioned before the Moncada attack. When Batista heard the song, Castro was put in solitary confinement. There he spent twelve to fourteen hours a day reading, writing letters, and watching the ants, flies, mosquitoes, and spiders. "A battle is always raging among the little creatures," he wrote; "the flies fight it out with the mosquitoes, the spiders catch flies, and the tiny ants carry off the leftovers like small vultures. The cell, cramped and narrow for me, is an enormous world for them."

Frustrating and isolating as prison was, it strengthened Castro's resolve. "This prison is a terrific classroom," he wrote. "I can shape my view of the world in here, and figure out the meaning of my life.... I feel my belief in sacrifice and struggle getting stronger.... I would honestly love to revolutionize this country from one end to the other."

Listening to the radio one day in July, Castro heard the startling news that his wife, Mirta Díaz-Balart, had been let go from her job at the Ministry of the Interior. At first Castro couldn't believe that Mirta had taken a job with the Batista government; he thought it was a lie intended to ruin him politically. Then he was angry at his brother-in-law, Rafael, who had indeed put Mirta on the payroll for one hundred *pesos* a month (about one hundred dollars) while Fidel was in prison.

Later, his sister Lidia came to tell Castro that Mirta wanted a divorce. Fidel had left her and his son without income, dependent on her politically conservative family. Despite his lack of attention to his family, Fidel seemed saddened by the divorce, which occurred within a year. He went to great lengths to keep in touch with Fidelito, who was now five.

The Moncadistas were released in May 1955, after a public amnesty campaign. Batista seemed to regard Castro as merely a nuisance, but not a nuisance he would allow to operate openly. Fidel was banned from talking on the radio or at public meetings, and the journal he wrote for was closed down. Convinced he could not launch the resistance within Cuba himself, Castro developed the 26th of July Movement. The movement was named after the date of the Moncada-Bayamo attack. Castro turned it over to Frank País, a young Baptist schoolteacher in Oriente, and then left for Mexico to prepare for an invasion. He promised that in the year 1956, "we will either be free or martyrs."

Castro spent one and a half years in Mexico preparing to topple Batista by launching guerrilla warfare in the Sierra Maestra. He raised funds in the United States, communicated with the 26th of July Movement in Cuba, wrote manifestos, bought weapons, and trained revolutionaries.

One new recruit was a young doctor, Ernesto Guevara Lynch,

known as "Che" Guevara. "Che," the Argentine equivalent of "Hey, man," was sprinkled throughout his speech, so that's what the Cubans called him. Guevara, who considered himself a Marxist, had left his native Argentina after medical school and traveled around Latin America in search of a revolution. He was in Guatemala when the U.S. Central Intelligence Agency (CIA) overthrew the progressive, democratically elected government of Jacobo Arbenz Guzmán. The experience embittered him against the United States. When Raúl introduced Che to Fidel early in 1956, the two men talked for ten hours. Che had found a revolution to join.

As the end of the year approached, Castro was determined to keep his promise to return in 1956. Even though Frank País urged delay because he could not produce a national uprising in time, Fidel was in a hurry. He had been arrested by the Mexican government for gathering arms and spent three months in jail; the valuable hidden supply of arms had been seized; and he had been warned that the Cuban government would ask the Mexican government to move against him again. So he bought a fifty-eight foot yacht badly in need of repair. In the middle of the night on November 25, despite storm warnings and rain, the yacht *Granma* cast off from Tuxpan on the Gulf of Mexico. Eighty-two followers—Fidelistas— were loaded into a leaking boat that could safely carry twenty-five. Guerrilla war had begun.

# 5

# THE
# SIERRA
# WAR

The *Granma* spent seven days crossing the Gulf of Mexico and the Caribbean Sea to reach the southwestern coast of Oriente province. The crossing was marked by storms and heavy seas, bouts of seasickness, and frantic bailing to keep afloat. The crew lived on chocolate bars and ham as they were blown off course. On November 30, 1956, the day Castro had planned to land, he heard on the radio of the attacks led by Frank País on military buildings in Santiago. The 26th of July Movement took control of the city for a day but was unable to hold on. País was the only leader to answer Fidel's call for island-wide uprisings to coincide with the *Granma*'s landing.

Two days later the *Granma* ran aground in shallow water, one hundred yards from shore and south of the intended landing spot. After jumping into the water with rifles held high and sinking into the muddy bottom, the men spent more than two hours floundering through a swamp of mangrove roots before they reached solid ground. Their heavy weapons, equipment, and supplies were left on board. "This wasn't a landing, it was a shipwreck," wrote Che Guevara in his *Reminiscences*.

Batista knew within two hours that Castro was back in Cuba. After struggling ashore, the men found a peasant who shared his small hut and food with them, but a Cuban navy patrol boat found the stranded *Granma* and began bombing the mangrove swamp. Fidel ordered a march into the hills. An American correspondent for United Press International (UPI) in Havana soon reported that Castro and his men had been killed as they landed.

Actually, Fidel's exhausted band was headed toward the foothills of the Sierra Maestra, thirty miles away. They were without food, fresh water, shelter, ammunition, or knowledge of the land. Celia Sánchez, daughter of a local doctor, had arranged for trucks, additional supplies, and more men to meet the expedition near Niquero, but the *Granma* had not landed there, as intended. After three days and two nights covering twenty-two miles, the Fidelistas were resting on a low hillside near a cane field, in a place called Alegría del Pio, when they were ambushed by government soldiers. A peasant had betrayed their location.

As their position was strafed by planes, Fidel gave the order to disperse. Crawling away under the sugarcane straw with two companions, Fidel knew complete military defeat for the second time in his life, but he did not admit it. Three men were killed during the battle; twenty-two were executed within a day or two of capture; twenty-three were imprisoned; and nineteen simply vanished, having seen enough of guerrilla warfare. The fifteen remaining scattered.

Fidel and his two companions hid in the cane fields for five days. A peasant named Guillermo García, whom Celia Sánchez had recruited, had seen the attack from a distance. When the soldiers

One of Castro's closest advisers in the Sierra Maestra and afterwards was Ernesto Guevara Lynch (right). He is known to history as "Che."

left, he began looking for survivors and helped guide Castro and the two with him thirty-five miles northeast to the farmhouse of another friendly peasant.

At the farmhouse the four were joined by Raúl and four others. One more rebel straggled in and then six, including Che Guevara. Eventually sixteen men, including Guillermo, reassembled, and Castro told them with his unfailing confidence: "We're going to win." Four new peasants were recruited and more weapons were delivered from the movement in Santiago.

Slowly the rebel band made its way into the Sierra Maestra, a tree- and bush-covered jungle some eighty miles long, thirty-five to forty miles wide, and six thousand feet at its highest point. Fidel was convinced that Oriente, with its tradition of rebellion, was the best place for a guerrilla war. There he could follow in the footsteps of such Cuban heroes as Gómez, Martí, and Maceo, using the tactics they had invented.

The first few weeks of the two-year war were the hardest, although Batista paid them little attention. He really did think Castro and his group had been wiped out. The men endured great physical hardship and great hunger. Their hair grew long and their clothes became filthy. Without the necessary implements to shave, they turned into *barbudos* or bearded ones.

As they learned to survive in the mountains, the Fidelistas gained support from the peasants. Castro had grown up among peasants and sugarcane workers; he knew how to talk to them and inspire their loyalty. The rebels worked with peasants on farm chores, stopping to harvest the coffee when necessary. They paid for food and supplies. Eventually, Che set up a clinic, providing the first medical care ever in the mountains. Schools were started for the children, but illiterate adults came, too. By the end of the war, there were thirty such schools.

In return the peasants hid and protected the rebels. They became guides for pack trains, which brought food, arms, and ammunition into the mountains from the urban guerrillas. The peasants also joined the rebel army.

Six weeks after the defeat at Alegría del Pio, in January of 1957, Castro's rebels had their first military success, attacking a small army post at the mouth of La Plata River. In a brief combat the rebels captured nine rifles and a submachine gun and munitions. For once they had more weapons than men. Captured and wounded soldiers were given medical attention and released, establishing a precedent that stood in stark contrast to Batista's policy of torturing and executing captured rebels.

## CASTRO BECOMES KNOWN TO THE WORLD

Since most of the Cuban press was censored, the people of Cuba were unsure that Castro was indeed alive and that guerrilla war had begun. After another small victory, Fidel sent word to the urban underground that he would be available for an interview by a foreign journalist, preferably an American.

Herbert L. Matthews, an editorial writer for *The New York Times*, was planning a vacation to Cuba and agreed to go into the Sierra Maestra to meet this reported rebel leader. At the time, Fidel had only one camp and eighteen men, but he gave Matthews the impression of much greater strength. When the interview was published in the *Times* on February 24, 1957, Castro became known to the world.

"Fidel Castro, the rebel leader of Cuba's youth, is alive and fighting hard and successfully in the rugged...Sierra Maestra," Matthews wrote, calling Fidel "the most dangerous enemy General Batista has yet faced." Matthews said the old corrupt order in Cuba was threatened by "the best elements in Cuban life." He described the 26th of July Movement as socialistic and nationalistic and "bitterly or sadly anti-U.S." No wonder, for he also quoted a U.S. company executive who told him, "We all pray every day that nothing happens to Batista."

The interview with Matthews was a propaganda coup for Castro. When Batista claimed it had never occurred, the *Times* published a photograph of Matthews and Castro together. The image of Fidel as a *barbudo*, a guerrilla hero of the mountains, was the image the world saw. By March he had the skeleton of a real rebel army, with one hundred men. After that, Batista was hard put to dislodge them. "We slip through their hands like soap just when they think they have us trapped," Che wrote to his wife.

Meanwhile, in the cities, several groups were working to overthrow Batista. The 26th of July Movement in Santiago was especially strong. Rebels led by Frank País jumped Batista's soldiers on patrol, seized their guns, and sent the weapons up the narrow mountain trails, along with food and recruits. Even people in the middle classes contributed to the underground, giving five or ten dollars a month to a friend of a friend of a friend who saw that it got to the movement.

Women were an important part of the effort. Haydée Santamaría was helping País. Vilma Espín, who once studied architecture in the United States, also enlisted; she later married Raúl Castro. Most important was Celia Sánchez, who went up to the Sierra Maestra, which she had hiked as a Girl Scout, as soon as she learned where the rebels were. At first she acted as a courier, a known and safe contact, but she eventually joined Castro's band, taking part in battles and serving as Fidel's personal assistant and trusted companion. Celia took care of all the details of running the rebel band, kept the records, and managed the money.

In Havana the seventeen thousand students in the heart of the city were natural supporters of a revolution. When the events in Oriente prompted the university to suspend classes, students were freed to make politics their main activity. They were represented by the FEU, which organized a secret, armed wing called the Directorio Revolucionario, with José A. Echeverría, FEU president, as its head.

On March 13, 1957, the Directorio attacked the Presidential Palace in Havana. They succeeded in taking over the radio station and announced that Batista had been killed. In fact, the dictator had fled in an elevator to the fortified third floor of the palace, which the attackers were unable to reach by stairs. The attempt on Batista's life failed, thirty-five of the attackers were killed, Echeverría was shot dead in the street by the police, and sixty to seventy others were arrested and killed.

The failure of the Directorio's attack strengthened the remaining 26th of July Movement. Within the movement, however, differences between those fighting in the mountains and those in the cities and lowlands began to appear. Fidel insisted that the movement's main goal should be support for the guerrilla war in the mountains.

When it was won, he wanted to set up a government to represent the workers and farmers.

Members of the movement in the cities had a more middle-class democratic government in mind. They thought the urban underground would be just as important in bringing that about. By provoking Batista into counterterrorism, they said, urban rebels were arousing mass support.

Underground work in the cities under the very noses of the military police proved more dangerous than holding out in the mountains. Every morning corpses were found hanging from lampposts or dumped on the streets. Frank País himself was murdered by the Santiago police on July 30. The deaths of País and Echeverría removed two powerful and popular leaders from the revolution. No other leader arose in the cities who was strong enough to counter Fidel's national following.

For the remainder of 1957 the rebel army expanded its control in the mountains. Batista's troops pulled back, attempting to seal off the rebels with a ring of army posts, but they were not successful. Fidel moved down from the high mountains to set up headquarters at La Plata, on the southern slope of the Sierra Maestra. There, a hospital, school, kitchens, workshop, newspaper, and radio station (Radio Rebelde) were established.

In February 1958 Castro began speaking over Radio Rebelde, giving the rebel account of the war to counter the news coming from the Batista-controlled press. He also used the station to announce a massive general strike, an idea of the 26th of July Movement in the cities and lowlands. When the call came, all workers were to leave work and bring Cuba to a halt. As a preliminary to the strike, Fidel ordered the burning of sugarcane fields to cut off profits that Batista could use to buy more arms. His own family's fields were at the top of the list.

The strike was not carefully planned, however. When the movement seized the Havana radio station on April 9 and announced the strike, workers were taken by surprise, and there was only a sporadic response. The strike's failure brought a harsh response from

Batista—one hundred of the urban leaders were hunted down and killed. After that, Castro became *both* the commander in chief and the secretary-general of the political operation.

## THE END OF BATISTA

From the spring of 1958 on, Castro emphasized all-out war. Batista responded that summer with an offensive called Fin de Fidel ("end of Fidel"). With ten thousand soldiers, armored cars, tanks, and trucks, plus navy gunboats firing on the coast of Oriente from the sea, the army set out to encircle the Sierra Maestra. They planned to close the circle gradually and then attack Castro's headquarters.

The peasants suffered heavy casualties. The United States had supplied Batista's government with planes and helicopters for "external defense." They were used instead to drop bombs and napalm on the countryside. When Fidel witnessed the death of a close friend's child, he wrote to Celia Sánchez: "When I saw the rockets firing.... at María's house, I swore to myself that Americans were going to pay dearly for what they are doing...."

At the time, Castro had only three hundred armed men divided into small harassing patrols. What they lacked in numbers, however, they made up for with first-rate intelligence on the army's movements, brilliant tactical leadership, courage, skill in mountain fighting, and spirit. "They never know where we are, but we always know where they are," the guerrillas said. Firing down from the crest of the mountains, they were able to beat back the offensive.

After seventy-six days of fighting and the beginning of the summer rains, Batista's troops had lost one thousand soldiers who were killed or wounded. From then on Batista's defeat was assured, although he lasted another six months. In the cities, civic and professional groups were unhappy with the violence they saw. Honest, patriotic elements of the army, too, were questioning their role in support of Batista. Disturbed by Batista's violence in the cities, the United States had announced an arms embargo in March 1958. The action was too late to prevent the use of U.S. weapons in the summer fighting but was effective as a sign of disapproval. The Catholic Church called on Batista to step down, but he insisted that things were under control.

Fidel decided to move down out of the mountains with his own offensive. In August 1958 Che Guevara and Camilo Cienfuegos began marching in two separate columns across Camagüey province to the west. For several weeks they endured extraordinary hardship, fighting their way through the provinces, walking through swamps, swimming rivers, and starving most of the time. Together they managed to seize large areas of the island with only 230 men.

Meanwhile, Fidel and Raúl moved down to surround Santiago. By New Year's Eve, Che had captured Santa Clara in the center of the island; Che and Camilo were poised to march farther west to Havana. Raúl had taken Caimanera, just across the bay from the U.S. naval base at Guantánamo, and was on the outskirts of Santiago. Fidel was ready to attack Moncada once again, this time with a much greater chance of success.

In Havana, Batista told a few friends he was leaving. He turned over command of the army, appointed a provisional president, and boarded a plane for the Dominican Republic at 2:10 A.M. on the morning of January 1, 1959.

News of Batista's flight reached Castro that same day. Over the radio he announced that he would continue fighting until the army surrendered, and he called on the working classes to strike to prevent a military government. Remembering the looting and rioting he had seen in Bogotá in 1948 and the bloody reprisals after the overthrow of the Machado dictatorship in the 1930s, he urged Cubans not to seek revenge.

Before dawn on January 2, Fidel's car drove unhindered into the Moncada barracks. That afternoon Camilo Cienfuegos occupied Camp Columbia in Havana. In a speech before a huge crowd in Santiago, thirty-three-year-old Fidel Castro spoke about the revolution to come. He promised it would not be like 1898, when the Americans took over the independence struggle; it would not be like 1933, when Batista betrayed the revolution with his coup; it would not be like 1944, when the people believed they had taken power by electing Grau, who became a "crook." "Neither crooks, nor traitors, nor interventionists. This time, yes, it is a Revolution!"

Leaving his brother Raúl in control of Santiago and surrounded by his *barbudos*, Fidel began a slow, triumphal journey by car, jeep, helicopter, and tank across the breadth of the island on the central highway to Havana.

CHAPTER

# 6

# "THE REVOLUTION BEGINS NOW"

———

"**T**he Revolution begins now. . . . ," Fidel said in his first speech to the people of Cuba in 1959. "The Revolution will not be made in a day, but rest assured, we *will* make it."

Castro's revolution was a social and economic revolution that would "pull up the roots of injustice," as Che described them. Now in power, Castro's main goal was to improve the lives of the poorest Cubans, the urban workers and the peasants. First he had to explain the revolution to the people and build popular support for the changes he wanted to make.

When Fidel finally reached Havana on January 8, where his

rebel army and the 26th of July Movement had maintained order amid the general rejoicing, he was greeted with almost hysterical enthusiasm. By the time Batista fled, Cubans were united in opposition to him, but they were accustomed to following a leader, and Fidel was clearly the conquering hero.

The crowds in the capital were so great that it took Fidel four hours to travel from the Presidential Palace to Camp Columbia, where he was to address the tens of thousands, arousing their nationalistic pride. Several hundred white doves, which in Cuban myths represent life, were released as he began. By the time he finished late in the night, one of the doves had settled on his shoulders and was illuminated in the spotlight. To Cubans, this seemed a promising sign.

Castro spent the next few weeks savoring his victory. He roamed the streets in his jeep or car, talked to the people, slept only three hours a night. Still wearing his beard and olive-green fatigues, Fidel seemed unwilling to shed the role of revolutionary military commander. The responsibility of running a government was daunting.

## RUNNING A GOVERNMENT

Castro had named Manuel Urrutia president of the new government. (Urrutia was the only judge at the Moncada trial who had voted to acquit the rebels because they were challenging a government that had seized power illegally.) Urrutia appointed a cabinet, mainly from members of the 26th of July Movement. It was soon apparent, however, that real authority rested with Fidel and the several hundred rebel soldiers who had moved with him into the Havana Hilton. No one would make a major decision without consulting Fidel. At the urging of Celia Sánchez, he decided to become premier at the beginning of February.

Once he started running the government, Fidel approached it singlemindedly, with the belief that in order to succeed he had to be completely in charge. Celia continued as his personal adviser and

January 1959. Castro and his rebels appear before a Havana crowd after having seized control of the capital.

Castro's son, Fidelito, with his father in Havana in 1959.

detail administrator. She was the person who knew where he could be found, since he never stayed behind a desk.

Besides Celia, Fidel was advised by Che Guevara, the idealist intellectual, and his brother Raúl, the practical politician. Raúl has been described as "a calculating machine... Fidel multiplied by two in energy, in inflexibility, in fiber." Che was the purist whose principles were above compromise, but Raúl knew how to put those principles into operation. Both were committed Marxists, but neither was a member of the Cuban Communist party.

Celia, Che, and Raúl were the three people Castro could always trust. They replaced a traditional family life for him. Fidelito had been sent to school in Long Island, N.Y., during the last year of the war to protect him from kidnapping. He was brought by relatives to be hoisted onto the tank for Fidel's entry into Havana. Now nine, Fidelito stayed on in Cuba when his mother and her new husband moved to Spain. Fidel also reestablished contact with his mother and grandmother, who had been praying for his and Raúl's safety throughout the guerrilla war. His father, Ángel, had died before the *Granma* left Mexico. Fidel's brother Ramón continued to run the family farm, despite the burning of the cane fields.

In the first few months of 1959 Castro made rapid changes. He closed down the casinos, the lottery, and the numbers game. He outlawed prostitution and suppressed cockfighting, whose effects he had witnessed as a boy in Birán. He made stealing from the government a capital offense. Racial discrimination was ended. Most rents were cut in half. Construction was begun on forty-five new hospitals, mainly in rural areas. Workers who had been fired under Batista were given their jobs back. The land and property Batista supporters had left behind were declared to have been stolen from the people. Some $400 million worth of farms, buildings, jewelry, and yachts were recovered.

All these changes seemed to have no particular method or blueprint. Fidel made up a plan as he went along. He explained what he was doing in speeches that lasted four to six hours and kept Cubans at their television sets well into the night. In speeches before crowds, Fidel perfected the technique of a "dialogue with the people," asking questions that drew fervent responses. Disdaining elections as unnecessary, Castro relied on reading the mood and feelings of the country and manipulating that mood to his purposes.

In the first days of victory, Castro had told the people not to take vengeance on members of Batista's army or the secret military police who had tortured and killed their family members. Instead, he promised that the "criminals" would be brought to justice. Those trials began almost immediately. All in all, 1,500 people were tried; some 1,000 were acquitted and about 450 executed.

The executions were severely criticized in the United States, but Castro thought they prevented the bloodbath that could have occurred if Cubans had taken justice into their own hands. He found it hard to understand why the United States would protest these trials when it had never protested the torture and killings by Batista.

Despite U.S. criticism, the Cuban revolution made Castro very popular in Latin America. On a ten-day trip to Venezuela, Brazil, Argentina, and Uruguay, Fidel was greeted by immense, cheering crowds. At an economic conference on his tour, he urged the United States to give $30 billion in economic aid to Latin America over the next decade.

Invited to New York in April by the American Society of Newspaper Editors, Fidel used the trip as a public relations opportunity, trying to educate North Americans about the nationalistic hopes of Latin Americans. Time after time he reassured North Americans that "we are not Communists." He was disappointed that American leaders seemed more interested in whether he was a Communist than in what he would do for the people of Cuba. Although President Dwight Eisenhower was out of town on a golfing trip, Castro met with Vice-President Richard Nixon. In their brief talk, the two discovered they had very little in common.

Castro had gone to the United States seeking "only understanding and sympathy" not economic aid, but he could have used the help. At home he had to make major changes that would fulfill the promises he had made.

## REFORM OF AGRICULTURE

The Cuban landscape was dominated by estates with vast tracts of uncultivated or sparsely cultivated land. While the land was idle, people were out of work and the country had to import food. Since independence, the best land had been owned by American companies that had seized it or bought it very cheaply. Castro planned to give ownership of the land to the peasants.

In 1959—called by Castro the "Year of Agrarian Reform"—a law was passed to break up the large sugar, cattle, and rice plantations and redistribute land to peasants or sharecroppers in minimum allotments of 67 acres. The new law set a limit of 1,000 acres on landholdings, except for the most productive sugar and rice plantations, which were allowed to remain larger. In order to make it fit the 1,000-acre limit, half of the Castro family land of 1,920 acres was seized by the National Institute of Agrarian Reform (INRA), which had been created to carry out the change. Fidel's mother and his brother Ramón were outraged by the seizure.

Although the United States protested, too, agrarian reform was very popular in Cuba. Everyone was encouraged to contribute by donating tractors and other agricultural equipment to the peasant cooperatives that were formed to farm shared land.

Despite this support, agrarian reform was not completely successful. Castro had big ideas but little technical expertise or administrative skill. To provide meat to Cubans who had seldom tasted it, for example, cattle were slaughtered, but the herds were depleted in the process, damaging one of Cuba's strongest industries. The peasant cooperatives were not as productive as hoped; industrial machinery and scientific farming methods were needed, so the INRA moved to Soviet-style collective farms, with the land owned and run by the government. At the end of the year Cuba was forced to import 100,000 more tons of rice than usual.

The biggest question mark of all was sugar. Central to the revolution was the idea of making Cuba less dependent on sugar, a crop that required half of the best land on the island, provided employment for only six months, and depended on a foreign market. At first sugar production was de-emphasized in an attempt to encourage other crops. As sugar production dropped, however, Cuba had less money to import what the people needed. The island could produce sugar more effectively than other countries and earn fifteen times as much money per acre than from other products, so Cuba soon returned to reliance on sugar as its largest export.

## INDUSTRY IS NATIONALIZED

After agrarian reform came the nationalization of industries. Whether Cuban or foreign-owned, industries were taken over by the government with the goal of bringing service and profits to the people as a whole. American corporations had been using Cuban resources and markets to make profits for their corporations. The U.S.-owned Cuban Telephone Company, for example, had raised its rates in 1957 at the insistence of the American ambassador. In March 1959 Castro put the company under Cuban government management, expanded service, especially in the countryside, and cut rates back to the 1957 levels. That same month the price rates of the U.S.-owned Cuban Electric Company were cut in the rural areas to match rates in Havana. A national tourist agency was created to promote tourism, whose revenues had traditionally gone into private pockets.

In the spring of 1960 the Cuban government decided to buy the oil it needed for industrialization from the Soviet Union, at one-third the cost of oil British- and American-owned refineries in Cuba bought from Venezuela. On the advice of the U.S. State Department, the companies refused to refine the Soviet oil, so the Cuban government took them over. That summer and fall, Cuba continued to nationalize sugar mills, cattle ranches, utility companies, and banks.

After a year of agrarian reform, followed by a year of nationalization of industries, Castro went on national television at the end of 1960 to say that his revolutionary program had been fulfilled. In a country where 40 percent of the population was illiterate, the next year would begin one of Cuba's most successful ventures, the campaign for literacy. Castro declared 1961 to be the "Year of Education."

The government began the crash campaign by sending "literacy brigades" into the countryside. Cuban schools were closed for one year to allow students and literate workers to teach others to read. Ten thousand classrooms were built until the funds ran out. By the

One of Castro's first goals on taking power was to redistribute large tracts of privately owned land to poor peasants. Despite land reforms, life for Cuba's rural poor was still difficult in the 1960s.

end of 1961 the rate of illiteracy had been reduced to 3.9 percent.

In contrast to education, the economy was in trouble. In Castro's "revolution without a blueprint," there were many failures. Rents had been reduced to 10 percent of the tenant's pay; water and public telephones were provided at no cost; health and education were free; so Cubans had *pesos* to spend. However, they soon ran out of consumer goods to buy. Productivity was down, Cuba's financial reserves were drained, and foreign investment and managers were leaving the country.

Moreover, a third goal of the revolution, independence from the United States, came at great cost. The United States had always been Cuba's largest single guaranteed market for sugar, but as the

Cubans expropriated American property, the United States stopped buying sugar and imposed a trade embargo, banning the export of almost all American goods to Cuba.

Cubans could not shift overnight to economic self-sufficiency. Suddenly there was no steel, no tin, no paint, no screws or spare parts for factory machinery. Not only had all raw materials come from the United States, but factory equipment was adapted to those materials, too.

Cuba looked to other countries for materials and equipment, but in the process Cubans had to convert to the metric system, learn to make spare parts, and adapt factory machinery to imports from socialist countries. U.S. built plows, for example, could not be pulled by the tractors arriving from the Soviet Union or Eastern Europe. Cubans could build plows that would work, but parts for the tractors, such as roller bearings, still had to be imported.

Moreover, the thousands of trained individuals who were leaving Cuba created gaps that could not easily be filled. The first to leave had been Batista supporters, then owners of farms, ranches, and businesses whose property had been confiscated. Doctors and factory managers left, followed by teachers, accountants, merchants, landlords, and military officers.

## SPEEDING UP REVOLUTION

Castro's response to the U.S. embargo was to speed up the revolution, to move toward state control, and to seek aid from other countries. By the end of 1961 the banking system, railroads, airlines, ports, department stores, many hotels, movie houses, and bars, the sugar, petroleum, refining, telephone, and electric power industries were all publicly owned. State-owned plants accounted for 90 percent of Cuban exports. Thirty percent of the farmland belonged to socialized farms, as well as 45 percent of the sugarcane lands and 15 percent of all cattle.

Trade agreements were signed with East Germany, Poland, Czechoslovakia, and China. By September 1961 Cuba had diplomatic relations and trade with every Communist country, accounting for 70 percent of Cuba's trade. Some four thousand Soviet technicians came to help build hundreds of factories.

Still there were shortages. By July 1962 rationing of animal and vegetable fats, rice, and beans was instituted, followed by the rationing of consumer goods such as shoes and more rationing of beef, chicken, fish, vegetables, butter, and milk. Cubans received ration books with coupons to turn in for a limited number of the restricted commodities. Gradually, Cubans began to manufacture goods they had formerly imported, such as textiles, canned tomatoes, pencils, and dolls, then brushes, baseballs, refrigerators, and stoves.

After two years of improvising, Castro had a clearer vision of where he wanted to go. Although Fidel was describing the Cuban revolution to the rest of the world as a "humanist revolution," his closest advisers were Marxist. Fidel was clearly moving in that direction, too. He gradually gave responsibility only to those who were loyal to him and his idea of what Cuba should be like. When President Urrutia delayed signing laws the cabinet had prepared and made some anti-Communist statements, Fidel forced his resignation, replacing him with a new president.

Fidel also relied on the well-disciplined Cuban Communists. They had been very slow to support Castro because he never joined the party. During the last six months of the guerrilla campaign, however, when it was obvious Castro was going to win, the Communists sent an envoy to him and provided increasing support.

Communist party members were appointed to administrative posts, labor union posts, and army command positions. Che himself was appointed to head the National Bank. He knew nothing about banking, but Fidel needed a revolutionary, a scarce commodity among bankers. With Raúl's help, special schools were created to teach Marxism-Leninism to the Fidelistas and then to all rebel army units.

Cuban liberals were worried by the direction in which the government was moving. Major Huber Matos Benítez was a loyal veteran of the Sierra Maestra campaign who had become an excellent military governor of Camagüey province, the main cattle-growing region of Cuba. When Raúl was named the minister of the armed forces in October 1959, Matos and most of the army leaders in Camagüey sent in their resignations. Tipped off before he received Matos's letter, Fidel had him arrested. To Castro, resignation was an act of disloyalty.

"Either Huber Matos is a traitor or I'm a liar," he told his Council of Ministers. Matos was tried, but not allowed to speak in his own defense, and sentenced to twenty years in prison.

Others who had been Fidelistas felt alienated by the socialist trend. "I felt silence all around me," wrote Teresa Casuso, who had met Fidel during his exile in Mexico. "My friends seemed afraid to talk." By mid-1961 some 100,000 middle- and upper-class Cubans had emigrated. Many had lost property and income as well as hope for democratic elections and individual freedoms.

As Castro felt threatened by internal discontent and by the United States, the rebel army was modernized. A popular militia was created with 150,000 volunteers supervised by army officers. Militias all over the country became the backbone of Cuban defense. Castro also created Committees for the Defense of the Revolution (CDRs), a system of "collective vigilance." CDRs in every urban block, plant, and farm kept the police and security services informed of strangers in their neighborhoods or of citizens criticizing the regime. Soon there were ten thousand political prisoners in Cuban jails.

Thus, in 1961 Cuba made the ideological turn from "humanist" revolution to socialist revolution. Castro did not use the word "socialist" to describe his revolution until May 1, the traditional day for military parades in the Soviet Union. He announced his decision not to hold elections and to bury the liberal Constitution of 1940. If any doubt remained by the end of the year, Castro proclaimed then, "I am a Marxist-Leninist, and I will be one until the last day of my life!" And so Cuba would remain for the next thirty years.

# 7

# UNFRIENDLY NEIGHBORS

**W**ell before Castro announced he was a Marxist-Leninist, the United States and Cuba were on a collision course. Besides wanting to protect American investments and businesses in Cuba, the United States was waging a Cold War with the Soviet Union. After World War II, the two superpowers and their opposing forms of government competed for influence in the rest of the world. United States dominance of the Western Hemisphere was crucial to maintaining this balance of power between the superpowers. A communist country so close to Florida seemed intolerable. When Castro rode into Havana on a tank in 1959, the United States government was very concerned about the type of government he would bring.

Castro was equally concerned that the United States would try to intervene in Cuba, much as it had intervened after Cuba's independence struggle in 1898 and after the revolution of 1933. He also feared a personal attack. After all, the CIA had toppled President Arbenz in Guatemala in 1954. He was determined to assert military, economic, and cultural independence from his North American neighbor. Blaming the United States for Cuba's problems became a convenient rallying cry, too.

In that very first year, 1959, there might have been a chance for cooperation. The United States was the second country to recognize the Castro government and sent a new ambassador who attempted to talk with the revolutionaries. After Vice-President Richard Nixon and Casgro met, Nixon was certain that Castro was a Communist or soon would be and that the United States should overthrow him. America's fear that Cuba would become Communist and Cuba's resentment over sixty years of dependence, proved too difficult to overcome.

Castro intended, at first, for Cuba to be "neutralist" in its foreign policy. In this regard, he wanted to follow the example of countries like India and Yugoslavia and avoid alignment with either of the superpowers. Yet Castro was hard pressed economically and militarily as United States ties were cut. He was moving toward socialism, but the U.S. reaction impelled him more quickly into a form of government that would be attractive to the Soviet Union. The first contact with the Soviets was made in October 1959 when a correspondent for TASS (the Soviet government news agency) brought vodka and caviar to Havana and talked about trade relations and the possibility of diplomatic relations. Deputy Premier Anastas I. Mikoyan made an official visit three months later. An initial trade agreement was signed, arms were promised, and diplomatic relations between Cuba and the Soviet Union were resumed.

For most of 1960 the United States and Cuba engaged in a series of "tit-for-tat" actions that increased the tension between the two countries. The year began on a sour note. The U.S. arms embargo imposed during Batista's last year had not been lifted, and Cuba bought arms abroad. A French freighter bringing ammunition from Belgium exploded in Havana harbor on March 4, killing eighty-one crew members and Cubans. Castro accused the United States of sabotage in a speech that ended for the first time with the phrase *"¡Patrio o Muerte, Venceremos!"* (Motherland or Death, We Shall Win!). Although Fidel eventually took back the accusation (and no cause for the explosion was ever identified), he had already used it to stoke nationalistic and anti-U.S. feelings. Likewise, a Cuban army officer, Major Pedro Díaz Lanz, defected to the United States and then testified to Congress on "Communist infiltration" in Cuba. The war of words had begun.

Americans were already disturbed that Castro had sacrificed elections, an independent judiciary, separation of powers, and the rights of private property to his own goals. As Cuba proceeded with agrarian reform and the nationalization of industries, the United States tried to pressure the Cuban government by withholding experts, technology, spare parts, and especially the U.S. market. When Cuba seized three British- and American-owned oil refineries in June 1960 (see Chapter 6), President Eisenhower responded in July with a cut in the 1960 sugar quota of 700,000 tons, or 95 percent of what the United States would have purchased for the rest of the year. Right away Moscow announced that it would buy the sugar the United States had turned down.

"If they take away our quota pound by pound, we'll take away their sugar mills one by one," threatened Fidel in a speech in August, and he did. During the summer of 1960, most U.S.-owned properties were nationalized, including thirty-six sugar mills and two utility companies. Eventually, an estimated $2 billion in U.S. property was seized.

In October the U.S. ambassador was recalled, and President Eisenhower placed a ban on all exports to Cuba, with the exception of some medical supplies and foodstuffs. Then Cuba seized another 166 U.S.-owned companies, including Coca-Cola and Sears Roebuck. That December the Eisenhower administration made it official that the United States would buy no more Cuban sugar.

## THE BAY OF PIGS INVASION

During this cycle of actions and reactions, a presidential election was underway in the United States. The candidates were Vice-President Richard Nixon and Senator John F. Kennedy. The vice-president was depicting the younger senator as someone, who, if elected would be "soft on Communism." Kennedy responded that the Eisenhower administration had been "soft" on the Cuban revolution. He went so far as to call for aid to Cuban exiles to launch a counterrevolution.

When Kennedy was elected in 1960, he soon discovered that plans for an invasion were already in place. President Eisenhower had authorized the CIA in March 1960 to begin training and arming a Cuban exile force with a budget of $13 million. Since he had called for just such aid in his campaign, Kennedy felt an obligation to go along with the project.

Castro could sense trouble brewing to the north. Southern Florida had become home to a diverse group of Cuban exiles and emigrants. Many wanted to return to Cuba under a government more to their liking. They paid for private planes to take off from airfields in Florida and drop incendiary bombs in Cuban sugarcane fields and political leaflets on the towns. When that did not succeed, they turned to the United States government for more active support. By the spring of 1961 a group of fifteen hundred men was assembled, mainly the sons of well-to-do families who had lost much in the revolution.

Rumors of the invasion flowed out of the "Little Havana" district of Miami into the ears of Castro's extensive intelligence network. Fidel scrambled to buy arms, trained the militia to supplement the rebel army, and prepared the people of Cuba for the attack. "A revolution is not a bed of roses," he told a huge crowd on the second anniversary of the rebel triumph. "A revolution is a struggle to the death between the future and the past. The old order always resists to the death and the new society fights with all its energy to survive." In his speech Castro demanded that the U.S. embassy reduce its staff to eleven (the size of the Cuban delegation in Washington) within forty-eight hours. Two days later the United States cut off diplomatic relations.

The CIA plan was to destroy Fidel's meager air force before the invasion, to establish a beachhead on the island and fly in a provisional government of exiled leaders. U.S. involvement would be secret until the beachhead was established. Then the United States would recognize this government and send in military support, in anticipation of a massive uprising of the Cuban people.

In the very early morning of April 17, Castro received a call from militia units that the invasion force was landing on two beaches in the narrow Bahía de Cochinos (Bay of Pigs) on the southwest coast. Ironically, the bay was one Fidel's favorite places where he often fished. Fidel had also used the bay as an early model of development and had tried to improve the lives of its very poor charcoal makers. Castro built 120 miles of highways and roads so they could bring the charcoal to market. In addition, he sent two hundred young teachers to the area as part of his literacy campaign. As a result of these efforts, the people were very loyal to Castro and to the revolution.

After personally sending his planes to attack the ships unloading the invasion force, Fidel left to command the militia and troops at the front. Within twenty-four hours the expedition was doomed, surrounded by 20,000 men with artillery and tanks and no popular uprising in sight. Castro's troops captured 1,197 invaders, who were ultimately returned to the United States in exchange for $62.5 million in food, medicine, and machinery—the dollar value of the damage Castro said was done by the invasion.

The victory gave a great boost to the Cubans' national pride. For once they had triumphed over their huge neighbor to the north. Castro's popularity at home and his stature abroad soared.

The United States was embarrassed by the failure but did not give up trying to oust Castro. CIA attempts to assassinate him and to support a guerrilla force in the Escambray Mountains of central Cuba continued during the 1960s with little result. The United

States tried to isolate Castro diplomatically, too, expelling Cuba from the OAS in January 1962. As the Cuban economy faltered, President Kennedy decreed a total economic "quarantine" and tried to persuade other countries to cut off trade, too. Britain, France, Spain, Japan, and Canada refused.

After the Bay of Pigs, Castro turned more and more to the Soviet Union for aid and protection. The Soviet leader Nikita Khrushchev and Castro had met at the United Nations General Assembly in the fall of 1960, greeting each other with bear hugs—one tall, bearded, and thirty-three; the other rotund, bald, and sixty-six. At first Khrushchev was not eager to take on the financial burden of helping an underdeveloped country six thousand miles away. He saw an opportunity, however, to gain a political advantage in the Cold War and in the Soviet Union's disagreements with China.

After the UN meeting, Che Guevara made a trip to the Soviet Union and Eastern Europe and signed new trade agreements. The Soviets promised to buy 2.7 million tons of sugar, half the annual crop. Late in 1961 Castro's son, Fidelito, was sent to school in the Soviet Union as a gesture of goodwill. By 1962 the Soviet Union and European socialist nations accounted for 82 percent of Cuba's foreign trade, up from 2.2 percent three years before.

## THE MISSILE CRISIS OF 1962

Equally important as these trade agreements was the promise Khrushchev made to defend Cuba against any attack, with missiles if necessary. Castro believed that the United States, having failed with an expedition of exiles, was planning a direct invasion with U.S. troops. In April 1962, forty thousand U.S. marines took part in a simulated landing on an island off Puerto Rico. That spring Khrushchev suggested installing Soviet bombers in Cuba. The bombers would be capable of carrying atomic bombs and missiles with nuclear warheads to any point in the United States. The missiles began arriving at night in early September.

Castro believed that the threat of the use of nuclear weapons would save Cuba from a conventional attack by the United States. Khrushchev thought President Kennedy was young, inexperienced, and lacking in toughness and would back down in a crisis. The United States was in the midst of a congressional campaign, however. When intelligence flights over Cuba identified from thirty to thirty-five missiles (whose presence Khrushchev denied), Kennedy decided to act. On October 22, 1962, he went on televison to label the installation of missiles an aggressive act unacceptable to the United States. He called on Khrushchev to withdraw the missiles. He also established a blockade five hundred miles from Cuba that would turn back any ships bringing offensive military equipment. Twenty-five Soviet ships were steaming toward the line.

A six-day confrontation followed in which U.S. naval ships were poised to intercept the Russian ships. The threat of nuclear war hung in the air. Cuba shot down an American intelligence plane flying over the island. The United Nations Security Council met in an emergency session, but Kennedy refused to negotiate through the UN. The Russian ships stopped as they approached the line and turned back. Through an exchange of letters, Khrushchev finally offered to remove the missiles in return for a U.S. guarantee not to invade Cuba. Kennedy agreed.

Castro was furious that Cuba had not been consulted about the removal of the missiles, but in the long run he got what he wanted, a U.S. promise not to invade. In a secret part of the agreement, the United States also agreed to remove its nuclear missiles from Turkey, which is close to the Soviet Union. Despite his fury, Castro moved to maintain friendly relations with the Soviet Union. He went to Moscow in the spring of 1963 for a forty-day visit, and the Soviet Union officially recognized Cuba as a socialist state.

Five years after coming to power, the Cuban revolution had become a regime, protected militarily and aided economically by a strong ally. Castro's government had made some big mistakes, and the economy was still faltering, but the social revolution was complete. By 1965 unemployment had practically vanished, along with the "dead season" between sugar harvests, as agriculture was di-

**Fidel embraces Soviet leader Nikita Khrushchev. Castro came to rely heavily on Soviet economic aid during the 1960s.**

versified. The literacy campaign had been an outstanding success. Castro continued to command a great following. The Cuban people were for the most part loyal to the revolution.

Although the CIA continued to plot to assassinate Fidel (there were at least eight attempts from 1960 to 1965, ranging from Mafia hitmen to cyanide in milkshakes), Cuba seemed secure from overt U.S. action. President Kennedy and Castro even exchanged messages regarding the normalization of relations, but Kennedy was assassinated before his emissary could return from Havana. Relations between the two neighbors hardened into angry distance for the next twenty-five years, with Cuba regarding the United States as a bully and the United States regarding Cuba as an ungrateful upstart.

Several times relations softened briefly. In 1964, as the Soviet Union and the United States talked peaceful coexistence, Castro initiated a peace offensive, but it was rebuffed. Attitudes began to thaw again in 1973 when an antihijacking agreement was signed. In 1975 the United States voted with the majority in the OAS to end the multilateral diplomatic and economic sanctions imposed by Latin American countries that had been in place against Cuba for seventeen years. Then, in March 1977, the two governments signed maritime boundary and fishing rights agreements and set up interests sections (diplomatic missions less official than a full embassy) in the embassies of other countries in each capital. Each time, however, Cuban involvement in other countries—Angola in 1975 and Ethiopia in 1978—derailed the softening of relations.

Emigration also added to the tensions between the two countries. In the first three years of the revolution, some 250,000 Cubans (out of a population of 6 million) fled the country. Those who fled included physicians, engineers, managers, and professors. Immediately after the missile crisis, the U.S. government canceled daily flights from Havana, and Castro sealed Cuba's borders. Then, in 1965, Fidel suddenly announced that Cuban exiles in the United States could come in small boats to the port of Camarioca and pick up any relatives or friends who wished to leave. Regular airlifts were instituted for a period of six years, and another 250,000 left Cuba.

In the mid-1970s individual members of Congress visited Cuba. These visits were followed by cultural and sports exchanges. In addition, tens of thousands of Cuban-Americans returned to the island as visitors for the first time since the revolution. The last large exodus came in 1980 through the port of Mariel when Fidel again invited Cuban-Americans to send boats for their relatives or friends. Over 125,000 Cubans entered the United States between April and September, but the Marielitos included six times as many criminals or mentally ill as relatives or friends. A 1987 agreement finally allowed 20,000 Cubans to immigrate legally to the United States each year and provided for the return of criminal Marielitos.

The United States and Cuba show few signs of giving up their

In 1980 Castro allowed Cubans who wanted to leave the island freedom of passage. The refugees left the Cuban port of Mariel for the United States on small boats.

cold and occasionally hot wars. During the Reagan administration, Secretary of State Alexander Haig proposed to "go to the source" (meaning Cuba) to prevent the spread of socialism in Central America. The Bush administration clashed with Cubans in Panama in 1989, then anchored a weather balloon ten thousand feet above the Florida coastline to beam TV Martí with American programming to the Cuban people. Castro successfully jammed it but then signed an agreement with Ted Turner for a half hour or more of CNN programming a week. The U.S. naval base at Guantánamo, on the eastern coast of Cuba, is a constant irritant to the Cubans. Recently Castro has expressed a willingness to cooperate with the United States to stop drug trafficking in the Caribbean.

Although the Cold War between the United States and the Soviet Union came to an end in 1990, Cuban-American relations have not warmed. Castro's ambitious foreign policy and defiant stance have made the dispute between neighbors more complex than a mere backyard spat.

# 8

# AMBITIOUS FOREIGN POLICY

**W**hen Soviet Deputy Premier Anastas I. Mikoyan visited Cuba in 1960, Fidel took him to visit an alligator farm.

"You see that big alligator over there?" he told his guest. "That is you, the Soviet Union. And the fat one over there? That is the United States."

"And this," he said, holding up a fish to feed the alligators, "this is Cuba."

Cuba may have started out as a little fish, but under Castro it became what has been called "a small country with a large country's foreign policy." The island has had an influence in world politics out of all proportion to its size and population. From 1959 on Castro has seen himself as a champion of liberation movements, a challenger to imperialism, and a spokesperson for the Third World.

One reason for such an ambitious foreign policy has been to ensure the survival of his own revolution. In the face of U.S. hostility, Castro reached out to establish relations abroad and to secure economic allies. At the same time, the Cuban revolution inspired liberation movements in other countries, and Castro encouraged and supported such efforts. Throughout the 1960s he juggled his own ambitions for revolutionary leadership with Cuba's need for economic aid.

## CONSOLIDATING THE REGIME

At home Castro took several steps to consolidate his regime. In 1963 the Second Agrarian Reform nationalized all private holdings over 168 acres. This action made the state the owner of 70 percent of the land. The land was turned over to *granjas del pueblo*, people's farms, which used machinery, fertilization, irrigation, and other techniques to increase production. The government provided the tools and techniques and taught the people how to use them. Despite this mechanization, productivity went down on the people's farms.

In 1965 a new Communist party of Cuba (the Partido Communista de Cuba or PCC) was created, which Fidel headed as secretary-general. The appointed one-hundred-member Central Committee of the party had many former members of the 26th of July Movement. The party, whose members were all loyal to Fidel, became the ruling body.

In 1968 Castro took another step toward centralizing power when he nationalized more than 58,000 businesses. These included everything from taxis, corner coffee shops, and auto repair shops to street vendors and hot dog stands. Castro seemed to make the change for purely ideological reasons. "We did not make a Revolution . . . to establish the right for somebody to make two hundred pesos selling rum, or fifty pesos selling fried eggs or omelets.... ," he told the people.

With these steps, the state controlled 90 percent of the economy. Cuba became more centralized, with all plans and decisions made by the government. It did not become more self-sufficient, however. A request for a glass of water in a government-owned restaurant, for example, was usually ignored because the waiter was not obligated to do the extra work. "I went down to the old tropical market," wrote Carlos Franqui, a member of the 26th of July Movement, "but it didn't exist any more. No more fish. No more fruit. No more flowers. Where was it all? The socialist market was empty, bureaucratic, and ugly." By 1968 the economy was near collapse.

Cuba needed to develop industries that could manufacture goods for export, but the government had no capital to set up such factories. In an attempt to gain revenue, Castro asked the people to produce a record sugar crop. Starting from a production of 3.8 million tons in 1963, he set a goal of 10 million tons by 1970. Cane planting and cutting became an obsession, with everyone urged to do "voluntary" work on the harvest on weekends. Even brigades of foreign visitors came to cut cane. A harvest of 8.5 million tons was achieved in 1970, but the people were exhausted.

Thus the face Cuba turned abroad had mixed failures and successes. Production per capita was down, as a result of poor planning, the emigration of managers, the U.S. blockade, and, as cane cutters moved to the cities, a shortage of workers in agriculture. On the other hand, nearly everyone was working. The people were adequately clothed and fed. With more *pesos* than ever spent on health care, public health improved. Cuba became a model for other underdeveloped countries in providing work, housing, food, education, and health care to the masses.

## EXPORTING REVOLUTION

As described in Chapter 7, the United States was determined that Cuba's socialist example spread no farther in Latin America.

Cuba's economy suffered in the 1960s and food shortages were common. The sign in this butcher's shop reads: "Meat until Monday at 11 A.M. You lose if you don't pick it up. We do not open Saturday afternoon."

In March 1961, only a month before the Bay of Pigs invasion, President Kennedy announced the Alliance for Progress. He committed $125 billion in economic aid to Latin American countries over the next decade. After offering aid in one hand, the United States asked OAS members to impose mandatory sanctions and break diplomatic relations with Cuba in 1964. All except Mexico complied.

With a failing economy and isolation in the Western Hemisphere, Cuba became more dependent on Soviet support. At first Castro did not let this dependence interfere with his desire to support revolution elsewhere. Encouraging other revolutions in Latin America made strategic sense for Cuba—the country needed allies—but it was also close to Castro's heart. It was the responsibility of a triumphant revolution, he believed, to help revolution along elsewhere. "The duty of a revolutionary is to make revolution," Che Guevara had written in his manual *Guerrilla Warfare*. Castro did not think that revolution could be exported unless the conditions in a country were right.

Fidel himself was happiest as a revolutionary, but he was firmly committed to being in charge of the Cuban government. In his place, he sent Che Guevara on a global crusade. Leaving Cuba, Che went to Africa, where he took command of two hundred Cuban fighters who assisted rebel forces in the Congo. That experience was not successful, however, and he returned to Cuba in April 1966 somewhat disillusioned. He would prepare next for a revolution-making venture in Bolivia. Castro put up $60 million and gave him rebel army fighters for the expedition.

As in prerevolution Cuba, Bolivia had a large number of peasants. The country was undeveloped and dependent on a single raw material, tin. Unlike Cuba, it was not ripe for revolution. Although the working class was politically active, there was no strong organization in the cities that would supply guerrillas in the countryside and organize popular support. Even the Bolivian Communist party was oriented to Moscow and gave Che's band no support. The Indian peasants were suspicious of what they saw as foreign invaders. By the summer of 1967 Che's original band of forty-three was cut in half by constant battles, desertions, and exhaustion. Meanwhile, the CIA had sent a Special Forces unit and set up an antiguerrilla training center for six hundred Bolivian recruits. In a final skirmish, Che was captured in October 1967 and executed, with CIA permission, within twenty-four hours.

Che's death was a personal tragedy for Fidel. Che had been one of his closest advisers since they met in Mexico. Always the idealist, Che really believed that Marxism would work, that workers could be motivated by ideals rather than money. Castro announced his death to the Cuban people in heroic terms: Che had "a spirit that was always alert, a brilliant mind, a vocation for revolution," he said.

Bolivia was the most extreme example of exporting revolution.

With Che's death and other setbacks, Castro lost some of his zeal for the effort, which was not having the success in Latin America he had hoped for. His ally, the Soviet Union, disagreed with the policy. As a nuclear power, it did not want to upset the balance of power by meddling in the United States' backyard. When Cuba criticized its timidity, Moscow delayed oil shipments and delayed signing the annual economic aid agreements. Castro was forced to tone down his bold words.

Moscow's strategy was having more success. The Soviet Union supported local Communist parties' participation with other progressive groups in obtaining power peacefully through a united front. In that way, a progressive military government came to power in Peru in 1968. Salvador Allende's socialist popular front was elected in Chile in 1970. Allende's Chile finally provided a friend and ally to Cuba in the Western Hemisphere. Castro visited Chile in November 1971 and stayed three weeks, enjoying his welcome.

Thereafter, Cuba reduced its revolutionary activity in Latin America and reached an accommodation with the Soviet Union. In May 1972 Castro made his first visit to Moscow in eight years. Besides trying on fur hats in the chilly spring weather, Castro talked trade. Cuba joined COMECON, the Council for Mutual Economic Assistance, or the Communist version of Western Europe's Common Market. The Soviet Union became Cuba's sole supplier of arms and of wheat for making bread. Ten thousand Soviet technicians and their families were sent to Cuba to start factories. In return, Cuba traded sugar, nickel, and citrus fruits to the Soviets.

## A POLICY OF INTERNATIONALISM

Castro also looked elsewhere for friends. Cuba was short on products to export but increasingly strong on human resources. After all, Castro had invested great energy on programs to educate the Cuban people. In a spirit of "internationalism," and sometimes for pay, Cuba began providing technical assistance to other underdeveloped countries. Doctors, nurses, teachers, and engineers were sent to thirty-seven countries, including North Vietnam, Angola, Yemen, Mozambique, Ethiopia, Nicaragua, Somalia, Libya, and Syria. By the early 1980s Cuba had about twenty thousand civilians abroad, including 7 to 13 percent of its medical workers. Several thousand foreign students were coming to the Isle of Youth (formerly the Isle of Pines) where Castro had built facilities for study and training.

The example of an underdeveloped country providing aid to others less advanced earned Fidel respect among Third World countries. In 1961 Cuba had been the only Latin American representative to the First Conference of Nonaligned Countries. By 1979 the Sixth Summit Conference of the nonaligned movement met in Havana, and Castro was named its chairman. He served in this capacity from 1979 to 1983. The ninety-two countries participating in the movement wanted to avoid alliances with either superpower. They hoped to address the economic concerns of the nonindustrialized world, sometimes characterized as the southern half of the globe.

Castro used his leadership role to call attention to the alarming problem of Third World debt, which was nearing $750 billion in the late 1980s. Latin American countries owed $350 billion of this, much of it to U.S. banks. Questioning whether a "stable world order" requires poverty in the Third World, Castro has called for the cancellation of these debts, fair prices for Third World products, and a worldwide reduction in military spending. The misery caused if countries attempt to repay the debt, he warns, will cause social upheavals.

## MILITARY AID

Not all the assistance Cuba provides to other countries is technical. Cuba has sent large numbers of combat troops abroad, particularly to Africa. Because of Cuba's mixed Spanish-African heritage and because Castro saw great changes coming in former colonies, Africa seemed a natural arena for Cuban internationalism. Cuban military missions were eventually set up in Algeria, Ghana, Guinea, the Congo, Equatorial Guinea, Somalia, Tanzania, and Sierra Leone.

Cuba's greatest military success came in Angola, on the southwestern coast of Africa. Angola had been a colony of Portugal. A popular movement replaced the dictatorial regime in Portugal in 1974 and decided to give the colonies their independence. As independence approached, the three Angolan groups that had carried on a struggle against the Portuguese agreed to coexist until elections could be held.

One of the three, a Marxist group led by Agostinho Neto, established a revolutionary government in the capital city of Luanda. Late in 1974 South African troops crossed Angola's southern border to attack the MPLA. Neto asked Castro for help. Castro responded quickly with a troop airlift, which saved the MPLA from destruction, stopping the South Africans seventy miles from Luanda. As the struggle for control continued for the next ten years, more than 200,00 Cuban troops passed through Angola. A regional peace plan negotiated between Angola, South Africa, and Cuba finally led to troop withdrawals beginning in 1989.

In Africa the Soviet Union and Cuba had similar aims. The Soviets were willing to provide arms and financial support for military adventures if Cuba would supply troops. In Ethiopia, for example, a military *junta* had overthrown Emperor Haile Selassie and established a Marixst regime in 1974. Neighboring Somalia invaded Ethiopia in 1978 with the unofficial approval of the United States and several other powers. In response, Cuba sent twenty thousand troops. With weapons, tanks, and artillery supplied by the Soviet Union, the Cuban and Ethiopian troops drove back the Somali troops.

In the 1980s Cuba's attention shifted from Africa back to Latin America and the Caribbean. Castro gave assistance to the Sandinista Liberation Front rebels in Nicaragua, after forcing them to unite in a common front. When they ousted the Somoza dictatorship in July 1979, Cuba sent teachers and technical aid and stage-managed the new government from Havana.

The appearance of more socialist governments in the Caribbean and Latin America impelled the United States into action. The CIA had taken part in a coup that killed Castro's Chilean ally, Allende, in 1973. While the United States was involved in Vietnam, Cuba's relations with other countries in Latin America had been improving. However, in the 1980s the United States used the threat of withholding military and economic assistance to force Ecuador, Colombia, Costa Rica, Panama, Jamaica, and Venezuela to suspend or "revise" their relations with Cuba. Cuba lost another friend when elections in 1990 turned the Sandinistas out of government in Nicaragua.

Grenada was a particular loss for Cuba. A socialist government under Maurice Bishop came to power there in 1979. Cuba immediately supported Bishop and sent more than seven hundred Cuban civilians and sixty-four military personnel to help build a major international airport. Bishop was overthrown and executed by opposition within Grenada, however, in October 1983. Shortly thereafter the United States invaded, and twenty-four Cubans were killed. The death of the revolution in Grenada was a clear defeat for Cuban foreign policy.

Despite its failures, Cuba has exercised much power and influence in world affairs for a country its size. For many years Cuba was the model and Castro the spokesperson for revolutionary socialism in underdeveloped countries. Cuba's confrontation with the United States was supported by heavy dependence on the Soviet Union. Whether Castro can keep swimming among the "alligators," whether he will maintain a vigorous foreign policy as Communist regimes crumble and the Cold War melts, may depend on what happens next within the revolution at home.

# 9

# LIFE IN CASTRO'S CUBA TODAY

**T**hirty years after Castro came to power, the revolution he made pervades every Cuban's life. Cubans spend working hours, evenings, and weekends pursuing activities Castro says are for the collective good. Generations are growing up with Martí, Lenin, Guevara, and Castro as their heroes. Fidel likes to say that the revolution was made for these children, but he can no longer claim, as he used to, that the present must be sacrificed to save the future. The future is here. What has the revolution done for this new generation?

The first goals of the revolution—providing education, health care, housing, and food more equitably to the people—are still what Cuba does best, although housing and food have become scarce. Remembering the children in his first classroom in Oriente who were "barefoot and miserably clad," ignorant and poor, Castro set out to raise the country's literacy level. The task in 1961 was to achieve "basic literacy," defined as a first-grade level of reading and writing. Basic literacy was followed by the "Third-Grade Campaign" for adults in 1963, then by the "Battle for the Sixth Grade" in the late 1960s and early 1970s. In the 1980s the goal became a ninth-grade education for every child.

In addition, forty university centers exist today, as compared to three in 1959. They offer free tuition and a broad curriculum. Whereas admission to universities once depended on wealth, now it depends on political correctness, membership in the Communist party of Cuba. At the other end of education, there are 839 day-care centers serving children from forty-five days old to age six. The growth in education has required the training of eleven times as many teachers as in the days before the revolution.

Castro closed private and parochial schools, such as the ones he attended, and made all schools public. As state-run schools, they serve the broader aims of the society, emphasizing science, math, and technology to meet Cuba's need for agricultural experts, chemists, industrial engineers, mathematicians, and statisticians. They teach the value of combined work and study—"every worker a student and every student a worker." More than a third of junior-high students and almost half of senior-high youth attend schools in the countryside. They live in dormitories, study half the day, and work the other half in the fields, producing crops that help make the schools self-sufficient.

In health care, too, the revolution broadened access, guaranteeing "the right to the care and protection of . . . health," in a new constitution. Free health care is provided through polyclinics. Because the cities already had good health care for those who could afford it, new hopsitals and clinics were built in the most remote areas. Although doctors are more privileged than most Cubans— they receive the highest salaries and first priority to buy cars—all medical-school graduates must spend up to three years in a rural area or overseas. Half the doctors left Cuba when health care was nationalized in the 1960s, but Cuba now has 20,500 doctors, one for every 488 people, as compared to one per 1,000 people in 1959.

Life expectancy has increased to seventy-five years and the infant mortality rate has been reduced to fourteen per 1,000 live births. Cuba ranks first among Third World countries in public health. Malaria has been wiped out, as have polio and diptheria. Malnutrition has been all but eliminated; it formerly affected 40 percent of the population.

Ninety percent of all dwellings have plumbing, and renters pay no more than 10 percent of their wages in rent. Housing in the cities, however, has become scarce and overcrowded. Young people have long waits for apartments and, consequently, long waits to marry.

Racial discrimination was greatly eased when private beaches, hotels, restaurants, neighborhoods, and professions were opened to blacks. The elimination of unemployment by guaranteeing everyone a job also eliminated competition for jobs, a large source of discrimination. Blacks have not held high offices in the government, however.

Castro has also made a case for the overall improvement in the morality of Cuban society: "We've eradicated gambling....Cuba is the only country in Latin America where there are no beggars.... Not a single child in our country is forsaken or goes hungry....all old people have help and assistance...."

## WOMEN IN CUBA TODAY

Before the revolution, few women worked outside the home. Most who did were maids, cooks, or prostitutes. The revolution changed all that. Castro saw in women an untapped energy resource for the revolution. Prostitutes were trained for other work such as driving cabs. Women were asked to join the militia, the CDRs, the literacy campaign, and the workforce. Through easier access to birth control, more liberal marriage and divorce laws, legal and easily obtained abortions, women gained greater personal freedom from fathers and husbands. As the education campaign progressed, women eventually made up almost 50 percent of the students.

Today women make up about 36 percent of the workforce. Daycare for young children is provided by the government, and offices open late so that women can shop before work. Women are given eighteen weeks of paid maternity leave, and their jobs are guaranteed for nine months.

Women have discovered, however, that such participation comes at a price. They are expected to do it all—work, take care of children and a home, attend political meetings, and volunteer for work parties on weekends. The Cuban Family Code of 1975 requires that both husband and wife share household tasks and child-rearing responsibilities. Few males have yet been seen hanging up their own laundry, however. Day care that was free at first now carries a charge, and there are not enough centers.

Nor are women sharing in political power. Haydée Santamaría, Melba Hernández, and Celia Sánchez took part in the guerrilla war and urban resistance but were not promoted to leading government positions.

## POLITICAL LIFE

The tradition of masculine control is set at the top. All political power rests with Fidel, who is surrounded by Fidelistas, loyal government and party officials. He is the first secretary of the Communist party of Cuba, the president of the Council of State, the president of the Council of Ministers, and the supreme commander of the armed forces.

At first Castro operated with a type of "revolutionary paternalism." In the 1960s he had a direct relationship with the Cuban people through the media, mass rallies, and tours of the country.

When the economic system faltered and the people became

apathetic in the late 1960s, Castro decided to allow more participation. A new constitution was adopted in 1976, which created, after endless discussion and meetings, a government based on Poder Popular, People's Power. Among the rights guaranteed to the people are a job, an eight-hour workday, a weekly rest period, an annual paid vacation, health care, a free education, care in old age, and the right to be free from discrimination because of race, color, or sex.

People Power is transmitted through five sets of assemblies, from the neighborhood level, where people elect representatives with a show of hands, up to a National Assembly. The new system allows greater participation by the people, but the National Assembly meets only a few days a year.

In addition to the government based on People Power, the Partido Comunista de Cuba (PCC) is defined by the constitution as the "highest leading force of the society," which guides its progress toward communism. Belonging to the party is the only way to gain influence or privileges, such as admission to universities or vacations abroad. Cuba has a selective Communist party, with only about 2 percent of the population belonging. A would-be member must be nominated at the workplace by fellow workers and approved by the local party.

A third element of the political system is the government bureaucracy, those scornfully referred to as the "men with briefcases." As in other Communist countries, Cuba has developed a class of privileged bureaucrats who drive German-made Mercedes Benzes instead of Soviet-made Ladas.Cubans complain, too, that the elite don't buy in the same stores or wear the same clothes as ordinary people.

Much larger numbers of Cubans are involved with the mass organizations—the Federation of Cuban Women; the Pioneers, for children ages five to thirteen; the Union of Young Communists, for ages fourteen to twenty-seven; and the Committees for the Defense of the Revolution (CDR), to which 80 percent of the population belongs. The CDR is a unique element in Cuban communism in the extent to which it pervades Cuban life. In addition to welfare tasks, such as administering vaccinations, mobilizing women for Pap smears, organizing blood donors and volunteer work, and patrolling the streets at night, the CDRs maintain eternal vigilance over the comings and goings of everyone on the block. Such observation and reporting on neighbors is the most disliked aspect of the committees.

Ten percent of the population also participates in the militia, highly trained reserve organizations perpetually prepared for defense. Military service is compulsory for sixteen-year-old boys, who must enlist for three years. Cuba is thus provided with one of the three largest military forces in Latin America. After training, youths may also become part of the Youth Labor Army, which works on agricultural and construction projects.

Life in Cuba requires constant participation. Those who don't participate, who become passive or don't volunteer for weekend work for the *microbrigades* that build new housing, schools, and hospitals, are regarded with suspicion. Loafing and absenteeism are considered to be crimes against the good of society.

Those who don't go along are forced along. "Counterrevolutionary intellectuals," "antisocial elements," loafers, and homosexuals find themselves in the forced labor battalions, Military Units for Aid to Production (UMAP). At times Cuba has held as many as thirty thousand political prisoners because Castro tolerates no disagreement. A fledgling human rights organization in Cuba estimated that there were between six hundred and eight hundred political prisoners in Cuban jails in 1989. Over the years since the revolution, one-tenth of the population has emigrated.

"The government provided some things—such as education and medical care," reports Arturo Sandoval, a jazz trumpeter who defected in 1990. "But it forgot about the principal thing—freedom for man to do whatever he wants to do."

## CULTURAL LIFE

Conformity in political life carries over to cultural life. In 1961

Castro offered some "Words to Intellectuals." Writers would be free to criticize failures and mistakes, he said, but they could not criticize the system itself. Poets and writers who did were arrested. Modern popular music was prohibited in a country that has given the world the mambo, conga, rumba, and cha-cha.

Art and literature became politicized. Most movies produced in Cuba, for example, are propaganda-oriented. "I went to the movies," Carlos Franqui wrote in Havana in 1964; "there were lots of seats for the Russian films no one wanted to see and huge lines of people waiting to get in to see the Italian films. People went crazy if they had a chance to see an old Hollywood film." Cuban television has been described as dreary, bordering on awful.

What has been written and produced since the revolution, however, is less imitative of other cultures and more concerned with local and national settings. A mass culture has developed. *Casas de cultura* (local cultural centers) have been set up to provide classes in art, ballet, music, and photography and a center for community theater. A national folklore and modern dance company have also been established.

Sports have flourished since the revolution. Athletes are encouraged from an early age, much as they were in European Communist countries. Children with talent are selected for local teams, provincial teams, all-star teams, and then the national teams. Athletes on the national team are considered to be the pride of Cuba. They are cared for by the state, although all are amateurs and also work at jobs. When the national baseball team of Cuba travels, they do not compete primarily for individual glory, for large salaries, or even to entertain the crowd, but to enjoy the game and reflect well on their country.

The system produces champions. Forty-six Olympic medals have been won from 1960 to 1980, the last time Cuba participated. Sports events are free in Cuba. Baseball, which the Cubans adopted from the United States, is still the most popular sport, with pickup games held all over the island. Basketball is second in popularity.

**Young Cuban Pioneers practice dismantling a Soviet-made automatic rifle. Nearly all aspects of Cuban life are regulated by the government.**

Religion, too, is regaining a place in Cuban life. Castro's argument with the Roman Catholic Church has been class-based. Before the revolution, he told Frei Betto, most of the Church's schools, hospitals, and parishes were in the privileged areas of cities, not in the countryside where 70 percent of the people lived. Although religious services were allowed to continue, when Castro seized Church land, expelled conservative Spanish priests, and absorbed the Catholic schools into the public education system, he was excommunicated, or barred from the Church.

Castro believes that Christian teachings and socialism have some values in common, however. "I believe that Christ was a great revolutionary. . . . His entire doctrine was devoted to the humble, the poor." Since he had a series of conversations with Betto in 1980 and 1985 and met with a delegation of U.S. Catholic bishops in

1985, a period of more tolerance between religion and the socialist state has begun.

## A FAILING ECONOMY

The most lasting problem in Cuba is the economy. One issue has been how to motivate people to work. If everyone works for the collective good, what happens when one person works harder than another? How would that person be rewarded? Or *should* that person be rewarded? Che had a vision that the "New Man" would work without material reward, only for the good of the whole society. There would be no need for money because there would be an abundance of free goods and services. Some rewards would be given, such as designation as a "vanguard worker," or vacation trips to other Communist countries, and the right to buy scarce consumer goods.

For a time enthusiasm for the revolution and the benefits received spurred Cubans to work hard against difficult odds. In the long-term, however, moral incentives did not work. Absenteeism and loafing became a problem, as did resentment between those who worked hard and those who didn't. "Señores," Fidel said to Cuban workers in 1966, "there is something that must be quite clear: the revolution is the abolition of the exploitation of human labor but not the abolition of human work."

In addition to poor worker morale, Cuba continuously struggles against its dependence on sugar. Sugar remains the crop Cuba raises well and can always export to trade or sell for other products. Castro has found no better solution than Cuban leaders before him. The harvest has stabilized at around 7.5 million metric tons a year and accounts for between 74 and 90 percent of all Cuban exports. More than half the crop is sold to the Soviet Union at prices well above the world market price. Although much of the hard work of producing cane is now done by machine, large numbers of cane cutters with machetes are still needed. At harvesttime, when the cane must be cut quickly and transported to market while the sugar content is at its highest, "volunteer" labor is drawn from factories and the army.

Sugar, citrus fruits, nickel, and fish are Cuba's most important exports. A fishing industry and shipping line have been developed since 1959, making fish available to Cubans and ocean fish and shellfish like lobster available for export. At the same time, the tobacco industry has suffered with the loss of its prime market, the United States. The quality of Cuba's famous brand cigars has also dropped as sons and daughters of the cigar craftspeople get scholarships and go to other jobs in the cities.

Constantly short of goods to export, Cuba has been desperate for dollars to buy the technology, spare parts, and consumer goods it needs and to pay its huge debts to the Soviet Union. One source of cash has been the reexport of oil traded by the Soviet Union for sugar. However, the Soviet Union says it will no longer supply such surplus oil. Another source of cash is the tourist industry. Tourism gradually returned to Cuba, earning $223 million in 1988. A current building spree to increase hotel space from three thousand to thirty thousand rooms aims to attract more visitors from France, Germany, Spain, Italy, Brazil, and Mexico. Cuba has also had some monetary success in biotechnology, exporting medical equipment and selling a vaccine to Brazil.

Despite these successes, the country remains underdeveloped. The government lives beyond its means, unable to pay for all it has chosen to provide. Life for the average Cuban has improved but is far from comfortable.

Food, though available, has been rationed, including milk, beans, rice, meat, and eggs. One roll of toilet paper per person per month is allowed. Clothes and shoes are rationed, too, and the plastic shoes made in Cuba are very unpopular—"they make you walk like a duck." Cars are old and scarce. One can, however, buy anything on the black market, items usually stolen from the government or from tourist stores.

These hardships led to some experimentation in the 1980s. Farmers were allowed to sell their surplus crops in open markets and keep the profits. Many food items were released from rationing and made available at high prices. There was talk of taking the government out of the taxi business and of ending the rationing of clothes and footwear, but Castro decided the changes were a mistake. A period of "rectification" followed, a return to tightened government controls.

Such hardship has had an effect on the everyday lives of the people. People are grateful for what has been done but weary, too, of propaganda, endless meetings, and sloganeering. Life centers around work, and the revolution is a part of every waking moment, including after-work meetings and weekend volunteer work, work that has become known as a little bit "voluntario" and a little bit "obligatorio." Fear of being politically "wrong" stifles the exchange of ideas. Freedom has been sacrificed to equality.

Although the people still like Fidel and support many of the changes made by the revolution, the excitement is gone, drained by the frustrations of daily life, the shortages, the constant calls for sacrifice. Trumpeter Sandoval said he was tired of pretending to love Castro's revolution and tired of the intrusion of politics into every sphere of life. Revolutionary fatigue is setting in.

Yet there are signs of pride and resilience. "We didn't import our revolution," a University of Havana student proudly told an American reporter; "it was won."

"Our countries are too poor to give men great material wealth," Fidel admitted on a visit to Chile in 1971, "but they *can* give them a sense of equality, of human dignity." Cubans have developed a greater sense of dignity and equality and a greater sense of self-importance as a people, but after Castro that may not be enough.

# 10

# BEYOND CASTRO

F idel Castro has dominated Cuba for more than a generation. He defined the opposition to the old order, he defined the revolution, and he defined the socialist state Cuba has become. Now in his sixties, Castro is an aging revolutionary. His beard is gray, his middle is thicker than befits a guerrilla, but he is still in charge, El Máximo Líder. His variety of communism hangs on in Cuba even as it collapses elsewhere. What will happen to Cuba in the next decade, and what will happen "after Fidel"?

The biggest change to come may be in Cuba's relationship with the Soviet Union and countries in Eastern Europe. Castro has made it clear that he does not like the reforms Mikhail Gorbachev is making in the Soviet Union. On his part, Gorbachev has signaled his unwillingness to maintain the level of aid supplied to Cuba in the past. Cuba has cumulative debts to the Soviet Union of more than $24 billion. Deliveries from Moscow have already begun to lag. The Cuban government announced cuts in the daily bread ration at the end of 1989 because Soviet wheat had not arrived. Future petroleum shipments will be limited to Cuba's domestic needs; no surplus will be available for reexport.

Nevertheless, Castro stubbornly refuses to follow what he regards as erroneous reforms borrowed from capitalism, which have no place in a Communist society. "Perestroika [economic reform] is another man's wife," he jokes; "I don't want to get involved." He emphasizes, too, that unlike Eastern European socialism, Cuban socialism is homegrown. "Cuba is not a country where socialism arrived behind victorious divisions of the Red Army." Cuba, he has vowed, will remain the "symbol of resistance." There will be no tropical glasnost [political liberalization].

Any loosening of socialist economics—allowing snow cone vendors to work as private entrepreneurs or farmers to sell their surplus produce at a vegetable stand—would bring political risks. Once liberalizing starts, it can be difficult to control, as Eastern Europe and the Soviet Union have discovered.

As the Soviet Union reduces its aid, however, Cuba's already lean economy will suffer further. Fidel has told the people they must prepare for a Special Economic Period. They can expect more food shortages, fewer consumer goods, longer grocery lines, and less petroleum to run vital industries.

"What problem is Fidel going to have during the 'Special Economic Period'?" a current joke goes.

"During the Special Period, Fidel will continue as Commandante, but Hunger will be General."

Castro seems to have run out of ideas of how to make socialism work better. He has always been better at military strategy and foreign affairs than running the country. A warming relationship with the United States seems clearly to Cuba's economic advantage, and it would be to the United States' advantage to involve

Cuba in seeking peace in Central America, but there has been no easing of hostility on either side.

At present there is very little organized opposition to Castro and very little space—geographically or politically—for it to develop. The Soviet media has mentioned the growth of a small dissident movement, perhaps fifteen groups whose platforms range from support of perestroika in the Soviet Union to freedom of religious worship in Cuba. An Independent Movement of Democratic Unity, formed in the spring of 1989, gave a hint of what changes some Cubans would like to see: separating the government from the Communist party's control, restoring private farming, cutting the country's military, revising the constitution to limit the use of Cuban troops abroad, and a national vote on Castro's leadership.

Gustavo Arcos, who fought with Castro at Moncada, now helps lead the Cuban Committee for Human Rights, which has just a few dozen members. Arcos thinks that "the idea of democracy that now seems dead in Cuba will rise again." Cubans may appear Communist, he told a *Washington Post* writer, but for most it is a pose necessary for survival; "a great part of the country is faking it. . . ." When this regime disappears, he claims that many who are now supporting Castro will push for democracy. He has suggested that all Cubans, both on the island and off, engage in a national dialogue on the country's future.

The younger generation in particular no longer listens to Castro's speeches and mocks him with a song that hit the top of the hit parade briefly in 1988, "This Man Is Crazy."

"Almost all of the students here want change," commented a University of Havana student to a United States journalist. "But no one wants to be the first to come forward and say it."

"The revolution was necessary," said another, "and in the first few years it did a lot of good. It gave a lot of people a chance. But now this revolution is like a handicap." The next generation is pushing to be part of the leadership, but the revolutionary generation is still in control.

Castro will find it difficult to change. "The most important feature of Fidel's character is that he will not accept defeat," his brother Raúl has said. He cannot blame the leadership of the past because he has been the leadership of the past. "Fidel Castro has never stepped out of character," wrote Herbert Matthews, who first interviewed him in the Sierra in 1957. "His role is that of a revolutionary, and he is going to go on playing it until he dies."

In 1989 four top officers in the Cuban military were executed for drug trafficking. Some say that one, Major General Arnaldo Ochoa Sanchez, who had been the military commander in Angola, was really executed because he was attracting a political following and questioning Castro's policies. As a guerrilla, Castro always feels under siege and reacts harshly to those who pose a threat to his personal power.

Castro has consistently been a lone wolf who never takes orders from anyone and rarely takes advice. The death of Celia Sánchez from cancer in 1980 deprived him of the person closest to him. Now "Fidel is surrounded by people who tell him only good things," said Jesus Yanes Pelletier, a Cuban dissident and ex-Fidelista. Castro still thinks, however, that he knows what the people want and that he is the best man to lead the nation on the true path to socialism. He is a grandfatherly figure to the Cuban people, but a crazy grandfather who has to be tolerated at times. "Everything here is old and aging," says Arcos, "including him and his ideas."

There is, nevertheless, no political successor in sight. Raúl Castro has been with Fidel since Moncada, but he is nearly the same age and lacks Fidel's charisma. Fidel could convince you that green is red, Cubans say; Raúl could not. Nor have government institutions or an independent party apparatus evolved. Cubans have always followed one strong leader, in the Latin American tradition of *personalismo*. Castro has provided a clear national identity, an accomplishment that is difficult to follow.

"There is a lot of discontent...," says a diplomat in Havana, "but Castro remains a very popular figure who is seen as being above the corruption and inefficiency which wear people down

**Cuban dissidents have been routinely jailed by Castro. However, a committee for human rights has been set up to urge a move toward greater democracy.**

here . . . He can still genuinely move people just by his charisma and force of will."

Castro continues to live without an income from the state but has all his needs met. He owns a Mercedes Benz and has a country retreat on the Isle of Youth (formerly called the Isle of Pines) for hunting, fishing, and skin diving. He also likes baseball, motor-boating, and dominoes, which he can play for hours. He seldom drinks but has been a heavy cigar smoker. No mansions outside the country await his retirement, since he would never leave Cuba.

Castro's own view of himself is that he has been "a man of faith, confidence and optimism." Less positively, his consuming passion has been to leave his fingerprints on the pages of history. The author of his most extensive biography, Tad Szulc, says he has been violent, given to tantrums, devious, manipulative, and defiant of all authority. He has episodes of depression and a tendency toward the tragic. That tendency is reflected in the slogan painted on Cuban baseball fields and the slogan that ends all his speeches, "Socialism or Death." For Fidel, there is no middle ground.

The winds of change may be blowing strongly elsewhere, but Cuba is an island. Castro has shaped it to his own vision. His inability to change is tragic both for him and for Cuba.

## TIME LINE

| | |
|---|---|
| **1000 B.C.** | |
| **–A.D. 1492** | Ciboney and Arawak Indians inhabit Cuba |
| **1492** | Christopher Columbus explores the northeastern coast of Cuba and claims it for Spain |
| **1868** | "El Grito de Yara" begins the Ten Years War for independence from Spain |
| **1895** | The Cuban war for independence begins again; José Martí is killed |
| **1898** | The United States intervenes in the Cuban war; Spain admits defeat |
| **1901** | Platt Amendment gives the United States the right to intervene in Cuban politics |
| **1914–1918** | World War I is fought |
| **1927** | *Fidel Castro Ruz is born in Oriente province* |
| **1933** | Dictatorial President Machado is ousted with help from Fulgencio Batista |
| **1939** | World War II breaks out in Europe |
| **1940** | A reform constitution is adopted |
| **1945** | World War II ends |
| **1945–1950** | *Fidel attends the University of Havana and graduates with a law degree* |
| **1948** | *Fidel marries Mirta Díaz-Balart* |
| **1949** | *Fidel's son Fidelito is born* |
| **1952** | Batista overthrows the legally elected government |
| **1953** | *Castro attacks the Moncada barracks with a rebel force; makes "History Will Absolve Me" speech; is sentenced to prison* |
| **1955** | *Castro is released from prison in a general amnesty; 26th of July Movement is formed* |
| **1956** | *Arriving on the yacht* Granma *from exile in Mexico, Castro launches guerrilla war* |
| **1958** | Fin de Fidel offensive fails |

| 1959 | Batista flees Cuba; social and economic revolution begins; *Castro becomes prime minister* |
| 1960 | Land reform and nationalization of utilities and property; United States cuts off sugar quota; bans exports to Cuba |
| 1961 | United States breaks off diplomatic relations with Cuba; Bay of Pigs invasion fails; *Castro declares Cuba a socialist state; launches "Year of Education"* |
| 1962 | Soviet leader Nikita Khrushchev withdraws nuclear missiles from Cuba |
| 1965 | New Communist party of Cuba is created; *Fidel is secretary-general* |
| 1967 | Che Guevara is killed in Bolivia |
| 1968 | Small retail businesses are nationalized |
| 1970 | Cuba produces a record sugar crop of 8.5 million tons |
| 1975 | Cuban troops sent to Angola |
| 1976 | New constitution adopted based on *Poder Popular*, People's Power |
| 1979 | *Castro is elected president of nonaligned movement* |
| 1980 | During the Mariel boatlift, 125,000 Cubans leave the island |
| 1983 | United States invasion of Grenada ends Cuban assistance to that Caribbean nation |
| 1989 | Thirtieth anniversary of the revolution is celebrated; Independent Movement of Democratic Unity is formed to urge democratic changes |
| 1990 | Soviet Union announces cuts in aid and trade with Cuba |

# GLOSSARY

**Alegría del Pio**   (ah lay GREE ah del PEE oh)   Site of first attack on Fidel's invading force in 1959.

**Alliance for Progress**   Economic aid program to Latin America announced by President John F. Kennedy in 1961.

**Bahía de Cochinos**   (bah EE ah day ko CHEE nos)   The Bay of Pigs, where exile-led invasion landed in 1961.

**barbudos**   (bar BOO dos)   Bearded ones, referring to Castro's guerrilla fighters who had grown beards in the Sierra Maestra.

**Batista, Fulgencio**   (bah TEES tah, ful HEN seo)   Army sergeant who became dictator of Cuba in the 1950s; overthrown by Castro in 1959.

**campesinos**   (kahm pah SEE nos)   Peasants.

**casas de cultura**   (kah SAS day kul TOU rah)   Local cultural centers that provide classes in art, ballet, music, etc., and a theater.

**Castro Díaz-Balart, Fidel**   (KAS tro DEE az-bah LART, fee DEL)   Castro's son, called "Fidelito."

**Castro Ruz** (roos)**, Fidel Alejandro**   (ah lay HAHN dro)   Full name of man who has been head of state in Cuba since 1959; Castro is his father's name; Ruz his mother's last name, which is usually dropped.

**Castro Ruz, Raúl**   (rah OOL)   Younger brother of Fidel Castro.

**central**   (sahn TRAL)   A large sugarmill.

**Céspedes, Carlos Manuel de**   (THAS pay thas, CAR los mahn WELL day)   Leader who began Cuba's Ten Years War for independence.

**Chibás, Eduardo "Eddy"**   (chee BAS, ad wah doh)   Leader of Cuba's Ortodoxo party.

**Colegio Belén**   (ko LEH yo bay LEN)   Jesuit school in Havana which Fidel attended for high school.

**Communist Manifesto**   A pamphlet written in 1848 by Karl Marx and Friedrich Engels giving the theory and program of communism.

**Díaz-Balart, Mirta**   (MEER tah)   Castro's wife whom he married in 1948 and from whom he was divorced six years later.

**Directorio Revolucionario**   (dee rek TOH reo re vo lu sha NAH reo)   Secret, armed wing of the Federation of University Students (FEU).

**Echeverría, José A.**   (ay chay vah REE ah, hoh SAY)   President of the Federation of University Students and head of the Directorio in the mid-1950s.

**El grito de Yara**   (el GREE toh day YAR ah)   "The cry of freedom"; a proclamation from the town of Yara in 1868 that began the Ten Years War for independence from Spain.

**El Máximo Líder**   (el MAX ee mo LEE dare)   "The Maximum Leader"; a term often applied to Castro.

**Federation of University Students (FEU)**   Large student organization at the University of Havana active in national politics; in Spanish, the Federación Estudiantil Universitaria.

**Fidelistas**   (fee del LEES tas)   Followers of Fidel Castro.

**Fin de Fidel**   (FEEN day fee DEL)   Campaign launched by Fulgencio Batista to put an end to Fidel in the Sierra Maestra.

**Gómez, Máximo**   (GO mez, MAX ee mo)   Leader in the Ten Years War.

**granjas del pueblo**   (GRAHN has del PWE blo)   People's farms; farming tools and techniques were provided by the government and the people were taught how to use them.

**Grau San Martín, Ramón**   (grau sahn mar TEEN, ray MOAN)   Leader of Cuba in the 1930s and president in the 1940s.

**Guevara Lynch, Ernesto "Che"**   (guah VAH rah, er NES toh)   Argentine doctor recruited to the Cuban revolution, leader in Castro's government; killed in Bolivia in 1967.

**Havana**   Capital and largest city of Cuba.

**latifundium**   (lah tuh FUN dee um)   A large landed estate, usually with an absentee owner; the plural is *latifundia.*

**Maceo, Antonio**   (mah SEE oh)   Called the Bronze Titan; leader of rebel Cuban forces in independence wars of the nineteenth century.

**Marielitos**   (mah ree el LEE tos)   Name given to Cubans who emigrated from the port of Mariel, Cuba, in 1980.

**Martí, José Julián**   (mar TEE, hoh SAY hoo lee AHN)   Cuba's most famous independence hero.

**Moncadistas**   (moan kah DEES tas)   Those who took part with Fidel in the Moncada barracks attack in 1953.

**Movimiento Socialista Revolucionaria (MSR)**   (moh vee MIEN toh so seo LEES ta re vo lu sha NAH rhia)   Gangster-led political group in the 1940s.

**National Institute of Agrarian Reform (INRA)**   The government agency that carried out Castro's program of agricultural land redistribution.

**Organization of American States (OAS)**   An organization of the countries of North, Central, and South America.

**Oriente province**   (oh RIEN tay)   Southeasternmost province in Cuba; Castro's birthplace.

**Ortodoxo party**   (or to DOK so)   A reform political party formed in 1947; led by Eduardo "Eddy" Chibas.

**País, Frank**   (pay ISE)   Leader of the 26th of July Movement in Santiago de Cuba.

**Partido Comunista de Cuba (PCC)**   (par TEE doh ko mu NIS tah day KOO ba)   The new Communist party of Cuba that Castro formed in 1965 to replace the old one.

**Platt Amendment**   An amendment passed by the U.S. Congress and forced into the Cuban constitution in 1901; it gave the United States the right to intervene militarily in Cuba.

**Ruz González, Lina**   (gohn ZAHL es)   Mother of Fidel Castro Ruz.

**Sánchez, Celia**   (SAHN chez)   Friend and assistant to Castro during and after the guerilla war.

**Santamaría, Abel**   (sahn tah mah RIA, ah BEL)   Rebel who was killed in prison after the Moncada attack; brother to Haydée.

**Santamaría, Haydée**   (eye DEE)   Sister of Abel; she also took part in the Moncada attack.

**Santiago de Cuba**   (san tee AH go day KOO ba)   Second largest city in Cuba, capital of Oriente province.

**Sierra Maestra**   (see ER ah mah ES tra)   Mountain chain in Oriente province; Castro's guerrillas lived in the Sierra Maestra while fighting the revolution.

**The 26th of July Movement**   Political movement organized by Fidel Castro in 1955.

**Unión Insurrecional Revolucionaria (UIR)**   (oo nee OHN in su REK shun ahl re vo lu sha NAH rhia)   Gangster-led political group of the 1940s.

**United Fruit Company**   American-owned company that bought large tracts of land in Central America in the nineteenth and early twentieth centuries to grow bananas, sugarcane, etc.

**Urrutia, Manuel**   (URR u tea a, manh WELL)   One of the judges at the Moncada trial; he was named by Fidel as the first president of his government.

**zafra**   (SAF rah)   Growing season for sugarcane.

# BIBLIOGRAPHY

## BOOKS

Aguilar, Luis E. *Cuba 1933*, Prologue to Revolution. Ithaca, N.Y.: Cornell University Press, 1972.

Betto, Frei. *Fidel and Religion*. New York: Simon & Schuster, 1987.

*Bourne, Peter G. *Fidel: A Biography of Fidel Castro*. New York: Dodd Mead, 1986.

*Cannon, Terence. *Revolutionary Cuba*. New York: Thomas Y. Crowell, 1981.

Casuso, Teresa. *Cuba and Castro*. New York: Random House, 1961.

del Aguilar, Juan M. *Cuba: Dilemmas of a Revolution*. Boulder Colo.: Westview Press, 1988.

Domínguez, Jorgé I. *Cuba: Order and Revolution*. Cambridge, Mass.: Harvard University Press, 1978.

————. *To Make a World Safe for Revolution*. Cuba's Foreign Policy. Cambridge, Mass.: Harvard University Press, 1989.

*Franqui, Carlos. *Diary of the Cuban Revolution*. New York: Viking, 1980.

————. *Family Portrait with Fidel*, A Memoir. New York: Vintage Books (Random House), 1985.

Geyer, Georgie Anne. *Guerrilla Prince*: The Untold Story of Fidel Castro. New York: Little, Brown, 1990.

Guevara, Che. *Reminiscences of the Cuban Revolutionary War*. New York: Grove Press, 1968.

Halebsky, Sandor and Kirk, John M. *Cuba, Twenty- Five Years of Revolution*, 1959–1984. New York: Praeger, 1985.

Halperin, Maurice. *The Rise and Decline of Fidel Castro*. Berkeley: University of California Press, 1972.

————. *The Taming of Fidel Castro*. Berkeley: University of California Press, 1981.

*Llovio-Menendez, José Luis. *Insider*, My Hidden Life as a Revolutionary in Cuba. New York: Bantam Books, 1988.

*Martin, Lionel. *The Early Fidel*. Roots of Castro's Communism. Secaucus, N.J.: Lyle Stuart, Inc., 1978.

*Matthews, Herbert Lionel. *Fidel Castro*. New York: Simon & Schuster, 1969.

Perez, Jr., Louis A. *Cuba Between Reform and Revolution*. New York: Oxford University Press, 1988.

Ruiz, Ramon Eduardo. *Cuba: The Making of a Revolution*. University of Massachusetts Press, 1968; Norton, 1970.

Suchlicki, Jaime. *Cuba from Columbus to Castro*. New York: Charles Scribner's Sons, 1974.

Szulc, Tad. *Fidel: A Critical Portrait*. New York: William Morrow & Co., 1986.

Thomas, Hugh. *The Cuban Revolution*. New York: Harper & Row, 1977.

\* Ward, Fred. *Inside Cuba Today*. New York: Crown Publishers, Inc., 1978.

Yglesias, José. *In the Fist of the Revolution*, Life in a Cuban Country Town. New York: Pantheon Books, 1968.

*Suitable for young adults.


**Magazines and Periodicals**

"After Castro: the revolution that Fidel fathered can only succeed without him," Saul Landau, *Mother Jones*, July-August, 1989, p. 20.

"Brezhnev with a Beard," *Newsweek*, August 6, 1990, p. 24.

"The Cuban Revolution at Thirty," A Conference by the Cuban-American National Foundation, January 10, 1989.

"Fidel's Top Brass Free at Last," *The Wall Street Journal*, October 8, 1990.

"Gustavo Arcos, Cuba's Embattled Human Rights Defender," *The Washington Post*, July 9, 1990.

"Semper Fidel" by Marc Cooper, *Voice*, May 1, 1990.

# INDEX

# ABOUT
# THE AUTHOR

Judith Bentley has written ten books for young adults, including *Refugees: Search for a Haven* and *Justice Sandra Day O'Connor*. She teaches at South Seattle Community College and lives with her husband and two children in Bellevue, Washington.

92
Cas

Bentley, Judith

Fidel Castro of Cuba

25638

$13.98

| DATE | | | |
|---|---|---|---|
| | | | |
| | | | |
| | | | |
| | | | |
| | | | |
| | | | |
| | | | |
| | | | |
| | | | |
| | | | |
| | | | |
| | | | |
| | | | |